CRIMINOLOGY

SAGE has been part of the global academic community since 1965, supporting high quality research and learning that transforms society and our understanding of individuals, groups and cultures. SAGE is the independent, innovative, natural home for authors, editors and societies who share our commitment and passion for the social sciences.

Find out more at: **www.sagepublications.com**

CRIMINOLOGY

THE ESSENTIALS

JAMES TREADWELL

2ND EDITION

$SAGE

Los Angeles | London | New Delhi
Singapore | Washington DC

Los Angeles | London | New Delhi
Singapore | Washington DC

SAGE Publications Ltd
1 Oliver's Yard
55 City Road
London EC1Y 1SP

SAGE Publications Inc.
2455 Teller Road
Thousand Oaks, California 91320

SAGE Publications India Pvt Ltd
B 1/I 1 Mohan Cooperative Industrial Area
Mathura Road
New Delhi 110 044

SAGE Publications Asia-Pacific Pte Ltd
3 Church Street
#10-04 Samsung Hub
Singapore 049483

Editor: Natalie Aguilera
Editorial assistant: James Piper
Copyeditor: H A Fairlie
Proofreader: Audrey Scriven
Indexer: Martin Hargreaves
Marketing manager: Sally Ransom
Cover design: Wendy Scott
Typeset by: C&M Digitals (P) Ltd, Chennai, India
Printed and bound by CPI Group (UK) Ltd,
Croydon, CR0 4YY

© James Treadwell 2013

First published 2006
Reprinted 2007, 2008, 2010 (twice), 2011
This second edition published 2013

Library of Congress Control Number: 2012939734

British Library Cataloguing in Publication data

A catalogue record for this book is available from
the British Library

ISBN 978-1-44625-608-4
ISBN 978-1-44625-609-1 (pbk)

This book is for Abi, Evie and my family

Contents

About the Author

Dr James Treadwell is a Lecturer in Criminology at the University of Birmingham. He completed two undergraduate degrees (one in Criminal Justice at and one in Community Justice) and also holds a Postgraduate Diploma, MA and PhD in Criminology. His PhD work was based upon ethnographic research and he is interested in all aspects of criminal conduct and has written about football violence, professional internet crime, hate crime, drugs and alcohol and crime and the English urban riots in 2011. He was involved in prison interviewing speaking to ex-military service personnel in prison as part of the Howard League's commission into ex-military personnel in prison, and has published in the *British Journal of Criminology, Criminology and Criminal Justice* and *Criminal Justice Matters*, and regularly provides comment to local and national media on crime related matters. He continues to undertake qualitative work with individuals who are actively involved in offending, and most of his work involves themes of masculinity; professional crime; crime in the night-time economy; violent and alcohol-related crime; football violence; organised crime; youth crime, and criminological theory.

PART ONE

INTRODUCTION

Core areas:

1.1   INTRODUCTION

When I first encountered criminology, I was keen to know more about what the subject involved. My introduction to criminology came in the form of a fairly complicated textbook that had been recommended by a tutor, which I purchased before the first term of my degree. As I tried to comprehend what was contained within its pages, I found myself gripped by a strange feeling of dread. I had never counted myself amongst the most successful or gifted students, and can acknowledge now, with perhaps less shame or guilt than I felt then, that I struggled to understand the subject. I can empathise with the difficulties that those new to this subject can encounter.

Criminology can be a complicated subject, and it is not made any more simple by the complex terminology that is used in the subject, the variety and size of the subject area. This book was first written as an attempt to help those looking for a simple overview that will help them to get familiar with the discipline. It was originally published as a course companion for Sage, and I was really pleased that a number of students and academics told me that it had proved useful in making the subject slightly easier to navigate. In this expanded and substantially revised edition I have sought to stay true to the original aim of making complicated concepts understandable, and if it manages that it will hopefully be of some use. I have, however, received feedback about omissions from the previous attempt, and so have included new sections and expanded parts of the text. The aim of this text remains the same: to assist those new to the discipline who are unsure of the subject and who are looking to understand the basics of criminology get to grips with some of the core issues – the 'essential' basics of the subject.

It is not intended to replace textbooks, journals and more specialist texts. It aims to make the initial stages of the journey in studying criminology a little less complex, introducing the theories and terms that are common to criminology, and doing so in a way that will benefit the average reader without much previous knowledge. If those new to the discipline can make use of this book in the initial stages of study then it has served its purpose well.

 The new and revised edition of this book is now also accompanied by a companion website, which is accessible at **www.sagepub.co.uk/treadwell**. The website, which contains resources for both lecturing staff and tutors and undergraduates, intends to complement and build on the material presented here. For example, students will find additional readings which underpin the core curriculum as outlined in the book, while lecturers adopting the book as essential recommended reading can access material and information that can be incorporated into lecture slides or module guides, which develop the themes of the book.

1.2 HOW TO USE THIS BOOK

The key to success in any criminology course is not simply to learn and use academic language. Nor is it simply to understand 'core' theories, although knowing the terms and concepts that mark out 'academic criminology' from everyday debates about crime and criminal justice is certainly part of the journey. This book will give you hints and tips about how to understand and use criminological theory, and how to apply and critique this theory when you encounter debates upon crime, criminality and the criminal justice system.

This book has been designed firstly as an introduction. Thereafter it will provide you with a guide that you can use as a reference point (to works that you should then read yourself). You should use Part 2 of this book to give you an overview of topic areas that you are likely to encounter, and build on what you find. Although there are summaries of the works of leading criminologists in textbooks, nothing can replace the knowledge that you will gain from making yourself familiar with the original works.

To that end you should not simply passively read the references here, but make use of them. In the first instance, having read a chapter you can then use the references in the text to inform your reading and look at the subjects in more detail. When you find references in the text you can trace these to the bibliography at the back of the book. Once you have the full reference for a book that you think will be useful to you try to trace the text. You can do this in several ways. The first stop should be your university library, but you can also use the internet and local bookstores to try and find a text. It is important that you do not come to rely upon one book, but instead learn how to direct your reading towards other relevant sources and material.

1.3   WHY USE THIS BOOK?

This book is also intended to help you to monitor your progress as you develop in your study. Progress will be made through reading and gaining insight, but it is also likely that you will have to prove your knowledge, and often this will require that you produce some form of written assessment. For that reason this book also contains sample questions. You can always use these as practice for the real thing; and practice will make you better.

The unique feature of this book is that it contains two sections (Parts 2 and 3) that complement and support one another and, if used in conjunction, should assist you in becoming a more informed and competent student. Part 2 provides an examination of 'over-arching' criminological theories (that is, those theories that inform 'academic' criminology and that criminologists use to support the arguments that they make) which are combined with more general discussions in the field. It is hoped that encountering both the theory and practice of academic criminology will help you to develop a more comprehensive knowledge of the subject. I will restate the point here that academic criminology and the theory that we use is never separate from what happens in the 'real world' of practice, and students should know not only about theory, but also about practices in 'the real world' of crime and the criminal justice system.

Part 3 has been designed to assist you in developing and sharpening the range of study skills that are necessary for studying criminology and is best used in conjunction with Part 2. It is intended to assist you in developing your skills so that you get the best from your reading, and it will assist you in developing a wide range of skills. However, these skills and your ability will only be fully rounded if you combine them with the academic knowledge and understanding that come from engaging and practising criminology, and therefore the aim is for Parts 2 and 3 to support each other and be used in conjunction.

However, most importantly this book should not be read passively, but should help you ask questions. A common complaint I hear from academic colleagues and tutors (particularly when it comes to students producing written work for assessments) is that students do not analyse, but simply describe, and this often is the basis for students getting low marks. However, I do not think academics always make it clear what they want from students. When you come to study a subject at undergraduate level, you are not just learning about the topic, the facts, dates, key names and developments as it were that mark out the knowledge contours of the discipline you are studying, because undergraduate study is also intended to develop analytic and critical thinking skills. This means that beyond learning the core facts, you are also being asked to critically consider and appraise the claims made by the theorists, academic 'experts', official bodies, journalists and others whose arguments you have encountered, asking yourself if the basis of these claims is sound, and whether they apply or are relevant to the situation you are examining. It is not enough, however, simply to include references to authors and summaries of their criticisms (though showing an engagement with the subject matter and wider reading is important and you must do this). If this is all you do, then you may be demonstrating knowledge and understanding, but you are still being descriptive. It is *you* who must be critical, basing your judgments, for example, on your own knowledge and observations, and on a balanced reading and overview of what other people have written.

Therefore, if there is one overriding piece of advice I would give to new students it is read a lot, but secondly, always do your reading and research in a critical manner – don't take everything at face value, and don't always believe everything you read.

In this book, I have attempted to highlight areas for you to consider, sometimes giving practical advice or making an important point or question for you to reflect upon. These features are intended to stimulate you and cause you to question the assertions and arguments that criminologists make; and therefore to help you develop 'critical thinking'. However, with that point in mind it is worth reiterating that it is not just the essential study skills and theoretical knowledge that are required to pass a criminology course, your hard work is undeniably the most important component.

1.4   CRIMINOLOGY ESSENTIALS: THINKING LIKE A CRIMINOLOGIST

Before we go any further, I want to begin with a consideration of criminology as an academic discipline. More specifically, ask yourself the question, 'what is meant by the term criminology?' It is a good question, and it has to be said that there is not a single accepted point of view in answer to it. As an area of academic study, criminology is an emerging discipline (there is no consensus about its origin). However, it developed into a separate academic subject from the early to mid-twentieth century.

Criminology is often held to be the scientific study of crime (though not all criminologists support such claims to scientific status – see below). As a subject, criminology tends to look at issues such as the nature, causes, extent and control of criminal behaviour, both individually and as encountered in society more generally. As an academic subject, criminology is interdisciplinary, drawing especially upon a range of subjects, most notably sociology (particularly what has been called the sociology of deviance), psychology and psychiatry, legal studies and law, economics and political studies.

Yet many people have views and opinions on crime. Indeed it can seem that crime is always in the news, and how to control it is a matter of intense political and public debate. Even so, many people are not well informed about crime and justice. The issues are complex – whether measuring crime or dealing with its reality, issues are often far from simple. Many crimes go unreported and unrecorded, and keeping track of people's 'criminal careers' or criminal behaviour is difficult, by virtue of the obvious fact that crime is very often a covert activity. Finding out what works in reducing crime – and what doesn't – requires careful and thorough research, and is often contradictory to what people believe, as is the reality of much crime.

Commonsense approaches do not always hold merit. For example, many people suggest that long custodial sentences should be given to criminals because they have a deterrent effect on those who are likely to commit offences, as well as on the offenders themselves. However, criminologists have shown that for potential offenders, it is the increased likelihood of being caught and convicted that has the greater impact on crime rates. This is but one example of how the reality as borne out in empirical research might counter the intuitive, commonsense position that many people adopt.

Any balanced strategy to control crime needs to be underpinned by a proper understanding of the underlying social, cultural and economic causes of crime (making the case for social sciences). Yet one concept missing from the above list is politics, and today, crime is inherently and almost necessarily a political issue. When I encourage students to think about crime, somewhat mantra-like, I recite one of my favourite sound-bites: 'crime does not take place in a void, but in a context that is always influenced by social, economic, cultural and political factors'. It is appreciating that context, and what it is at any given moment, or historically, that is core to beginning to 'think like a criminologist' and move from everyday conversations about crime to a position more in keeping with the social sciences.

Areas of research in criminology are diverse, but can be said to include the incidence, types, causes and consequences of crime, as well as social and governmental policy and regulation, social control practices and reaction to crime. Some academics suggest the term *criminology* was first used by French anthropologist Paul Topinard in 1879; others suggest it was properly coined in 1885, by Italian law professor Raffaele Garofalo, as *criminologia*.

What is criminology?

Criminologists are interested in crime and the way in which societies deal with crime. However, many people will comment on crime and criminals, and have opinions on the way in which criminals are or should be treated.

Criminology therefore can be regarded as involving a more 'academic' consideration of crime.

Some academics believe that criminology should seek to be 'scientific' or 'empirically grounded' (meaning based upon fact, observation or experience rather than upon a theory alone).

Whether criminology is a science in its own right is contested; whilst some academics have suggested that criminology is the 'scientific' study of crime, not all criminologists would support that view.

Criminology is a multi-disciplinary subject.

Criminology contains arguments derived from philosophy, psychology, sociology, medicine, law, architecture, geography and biology, to name but a few.

Some academics believe that criminology is set apart from other subjects such as sociology because it is concerned only with 'criminal' conduct that is prohibited by law. For example, David Garland (2002) has argued that criminology is detached from moral and legal arguments and sociological studies that are concerned with 'deviance' because it is concerned with crime, although his view is not always accepted.

Criminology can be considered as separate to what has been termed 'crime science', which is a discrete sub-strand of criminology that has emerged in recent years. Three features distinguish crime science from criminology: the former is uniquely focused on cutting crime; it concentrates only on the crime rather than the characteristics or motivations of criminals more broadly; and it is wholly based on 'scientific' methodology rather than drawing upon social theory.

With the above points in mind it is important that you remember that when we study crime we are not studying something that is abstract or irrelevant. It impacts upon people's lives (those people working in the criminal justice system, offenders and citizens). The work criminologists produce can give rise to or support ideas on which working policies and practices are based (even if that is not what the criminologist intended). Therefore it is perhaps important for those new to the discipline to remain aware of the fact that what we debate often describes or may directly impact upon people's lived experiences. For that reason it is worth carefully considering the terms that we use.

Garland suggests that the criminology that first emerged in the UK was developed around the institutions of control. For the first two-thirds of the twentieth century, this was fairly narrow correctionalism, with its stress on individual positivism. Then subsequently, and more recently, this has been replaced with what he terms the 'crime control complex', with its emphasis on situational crime control. It is certainly true that for the most part during that period the Home Office was the biggest employer of criminologists, and that much of the institutional academic training that developed around criminology and criminal justice was closely tied to the crime control mechanisms of the state. In the UK just 30 years ago there were no undergraduate criminology degrees, and the subject was taught exclusively at postgraduate level. It was not until the late 1980s that the subject was offered at undergraduate level.

In 1957, the then Conservative Home Secretary, R.A. (Rab) Butler, approached the London School of Economics about establishing an institute of criminology, but by 1959 the institute was established at Cambridge University, with Leon Radzinowicz becoming the first professor of criminology in Britain. Radzinowicz's brand of criminology, indeed his approach to the subject, was born of a philosophical belief that there must be a connection between criminology and criminal policy and that the study of criminology, shorn of the study of law and policy, is both arid and dangerous – and particularly dangerous when it ignores the wider questions of social and political values. It is worth remembering that many of Britain's early criminologists were all too well aware of the threat of the unchecked state, as criminologists like Radzinowicz (and his contemporaries Hermann Manheim and Max Grunhut) were exiles from Nazi persecution in Europe.

It is perhaps therefore unsurprising that Radznowicz believed criminology must always keep in mind the liberty of the citizen. While Radzinowicz often worked with the government, he was by no means an apologist for policy with which he disagreed, and was a fierce critic of the government on occasion. He made no secret of his dislike for criminal justice policy under Thatcher in the 1980s, and often expressed his opposition to official policy, criticising for example the privatisation of the prisons and dangerous offender legislation.

In the late 1960s a group of young academics including Stan Cohen, David Downes, Paul Rock, Ian Taylor and Jock Young established the National Deviancy Conference (NDC) which was first held in York in 1968. These academics were dissatisfied with the orthodox (and government-linked) British criminology and were influenced by American interactionist sociology. Many of the core practitioners went on to be involved with critical criminology and/or the Left Realist movement. The NDC was a radical breakaway from the Third National Conference of Teaching and Research on Criminology at the University of Cambridge, a move that Radzinowicz subsequently suggested was a deliberate slight to him. Certainly in part the break was one also born of dissatisfaction with some of the medical, legal and psychological assumptions that NDC members felt characterised orthodox 'positivist criminology' of those like Radzinowicz. The NDC sowed the seeds for a sociologically grounded criminology in the UK that was less tied to the workings of the state.

Criminology is often regarded as a social science, and it is almost always hard, and possibly impossible, for social scientific theory to remove itself from ideological considerations. This means that when you study criminology, you may not be able to be 'value free'. You may believe some things are good, right, proper or ethical, or that others are not. It is important that you consider different perspectives and look at issues in a considered way, asking probing questions about what might previously have been 'taken for granted'.

If you want to immediately see disagreement in criminology, then there is no better place to start than with the concept of crime.

1.5 WHAT IS CRIME?

It may at first seem like a simple question, but perhaps the first thing to consider for criminologists should be the question 'what is a crime?' The answer may seem simple, but in reality it is perhaps more complex than you might think.

When people talk generally about crime they often do not stop and consider what it actually is they refer to. As a criminologist, one of the first points to remember is that crime is not static or fixed, it constantly changes. Things that once were not criminalized become so, such as paedophiles 'grooming' victims on the internet, or 'stalking' a former partner. Similarly, activities which were illegal may become legal, such as consenting homosexual behaviour between men.

Crime also differs in terms of geography. What is a crime in one place may not be a crime in another, with different countries, and different parts of different countries having different laws.

Why does some behaviour become a crime, while other types of behaviour do not? Clearly we do not all have the power to make behaviours that we do not agree with criminal, nor do we have the power to remove the label 'criminal' if it has been applied to behaviours with which we agree. This power instead rests in the hands of politicians (who create the law), judges (who interpret it), and those responsible for enforcing the law. It is important to remember that such actions do not occur in a void. Public opinion undoubtedly can impact upon this process, as do other powerful groups such as the media. Therefore a key issue when we think about crime is power.

Most people would probably argue that a criminal is someone who commits a crime, or who breaks the law. However, everyone will break the law at some point in their lives, and yet, clearly most people do not think of themselves as criminals.

Technically, and legally, actions are not necessarily 'criminal' until conviction by a court of law. The problem with this, however, is that a great deal of crime will go unreported, undetected, or will not be prosecuted. For this reason the term 'criminal' is not the only one that you will encounter in criminology. The term 'deviant' is sometimes used, but rather than clarifying criminology's subject matter, this can also serve to further confuse some people.

There are identifiable differences between what we mean when we talk about crime as opposed to deviance:

- Crime — generally used to describe behaviour that breaks the criminal law.
- Deviance — describes behaviour that is statistically uncommon, marginal, and not mainstream, but may not be illegal or prohibited by law.

In reality the terms are not always used carefully and the distinction is not always apparent.

For how long should someone be considered a criminal after committing an offence? Society considers some criminal convictions in some circumstances spent after a certain amount of time, but in a wider society there are no such rules.

1.6   PERSPECTIVES ON CRIME

There is no simple answer to the question of what constitutes crime. Instead there are a range of different perspectives about what should be considered the remit or focus of criminological study. It is to these I will now turn.

THE LEGALISTIC POSITION

The legalistic position is perhaps a good starting point for considering how we define crime and what is regarded as an appropriate focus for criminological research. The legalistic position suggests that what constitutes crime is a violation of the criminal law. It is often associated with Michael (a lawyer) and Adler (a philosopher) who believed:

> The most precise and least ambiguous definition of crime is that which defines it as behavior that is prohibited by the criminal code. It follows that a criminal is a person who has behaved in some way prohibited by the criminal law. (Michael and Adler, 1933: 2)

Michael and Adler produced this definition because they believed it would allow for scientific study of crime. However, it may be naïve to assume that by using an uncomplicated definition the subject becomes simple. Crime is a social phenomenon that involves people in complex interactions. Therefore, while there have been criminologists who supported a fixed legalistic definition of crime, this trend has passed and few criminologists would now accept the argument that criminologists should uncritically accept simple violations of the law as defining what they study. However, one exception to this view is 'crime science' which tends unquestioningly to take crime as simply given and is concerned only with violations of the law.

SOCIAL CONFLICT

Sociologist Thorsten Sellin challenged the legalistic position. He argued that, as 'scientists' criminologists should not be constrained simply by legal codes:

> The unqualified acceptance of the legal definitions of the basic units or elements of criminological inquiry violates a fundamental criterion of science. The scientist must have freedom to define his own terms, based on the intrinsic character of his material and designating properties in that material which are assumed to be universal. (Sellin, 1938: 31)

Sellin believed that in a healthy, homogeneous society, laws were based upon rules of normal behaviour. People largely did not break society's laws because those laws reflected their views. To simplify what was essentially an extremely sophisticated argument, Sellin believed that the core component in crime is conflict between cultures. Crime is more complex than simply the act of breaking the legal code and arises out of competing interests between groups in society. Therefore understanding these conflicts of interest rather than unquestioningly accepting that crime is a violation of law was essential.

COMPETING GROUP INTERESTS

George Vold's (1958) work could be regarded as building on Sellin's arguments. Vold differed from Sellin in that he was influenced by the idea that the criminal law does not always reflect the values of the society. He sought to explain why laws were made and whose interests they represented. Vold examined conflict between interest groups in the same culture. He suggested that people come together united by particular interests, and the desire to see those interests represented. He suggested that when two groups had conflicting interests, they might be able to agree a compromise position, but alternatively one side might be able to exert greater influence and be able to gain the state's support, which might then lead to legislation against the other.

Vold's concept is interesting as clearly powerful interest groups are heard more than the 'average man or woman' on the street and may have a greater influence on those with political power. However, this does not account for criminal behaviour that does not arise from group interests.

CRIME EXISTS TO PROTECT THE RULING CLASS

William Chambliss's (1978) views are extremely radical and based upon Marxist theory. Chambliss contended that acts defined as criminal existed to protect the ruling economic class. Crime served to reduce surplus labour, whilst providing jobs for some people in the criminal justice system. More importantly, crime, for the working class, was a smoke-screen. It focused their attention on the criminal actions of some within their own class, diverting attention away from the exploitation they were subjected to at the hands of the capitalist system.

In *The Social Reality of Crime* (1970), Richard Quinney, an American writer, updated the views of Chambliss, arguing that the criminal law protects powerful interest groups. Quinney asserted that neither individuals nor their behaviour are inherently criminal. He suggested that the powerful decide on prohibited aspects of behaviour, which becomes a 'social reality' that people accept. Initially concerned, like Sellin and Vold, with societal 'conflict', Quinney moved towards a more radical standpoint and argued (like Chambliss) that the criminal justice system was a powerful tool for ensuring that power remained in the hands of the elite.

CRIME AS A SOCIAL HARM AND 'ZEMIOLOGY'

In his work *White Collar Crime* (1949) American sociologist Edwin Sutherland offered a definition of crime that had not previously been considered in academic debate.

In *White Collar Crime* Sutherland suggested that many of the crimes involving business people were not dealt with by criminal law but by regulatory and civil law, despite the fact that they caused harm to society (social harm). He argued that in order to avoid class bias within criminology, crime should be expanded to include any act causing social harm that was prohibited by any law (not necessarily just criminal law).

One objector to this approach was Paul Tappan (1947) who argued that it would be wrong to label any person or organization as criminal if they had not been found guilty of a criminal offence. Tappan argued that it is important that the presumption should always be that people are innocent until proven guilty. More recently, and more controversially, the notion of crime as a social harm has been further extended.

In *Order, Law and Crime* (1985), Michalowski argued that any act, even if it is legal, should be considered criminal if it causes something he calls 'analogous social injury' (by this he essentially means any form of social harm). This reasoning could, for example, lead to tobacco firms being held responsible for all the deaths caused by smoking.

More recently this view has been taken up by those keen to move criminology away from a simplistic focus on crime, such as Paddy Hillyard and colleagues. These academics have spearheaded a movement called zemiology (Hillyard et al., 2004).

Zemiology is the study of social harm rather than crime and gets its name from the Greek word *zemia*, meaning harm. It originated as a critique of criminology and the notion of crime. In contrast with 'individual-based harms' such as theft, the notion of social harm or social injury incorporates harms caused by nation states and corporations. These ideas have received increased attention from critical academics such as neo-Marxists and feminists in the last decade. Indeed zemiologists would argue for example that a narrow focus on crime excludes a focus on more serious harms. Many incidents which cause serious harm are either not part of the criminal law or, if they could be dealt with by it, are either ignored or handled without resort to it. The undue attention given to events which are defined as crimes distracts attention from more serious harm, such as pollution or poverty. Indeed zemiology shows that criminalization and punishment can inflict social harms, and argues that the criminal justice system has many stages which can inflict pain in a discrete manner: defining, classifying, broadcasting, disposing and punishing the offender. Furthermore, these processes create wider social problems and social harms, which can bear little or no relationship to the initial crime and cause excessive social harm and suffering disproportionate to the original harm that was caused by the crime. For example, jailing an individual for personal drug possession may lead to loss of jobs, family problems and a lack of employment opportunity in the future, in effect doing more harm than good. Therefore some zemiologists question the harmful practices of the administration of criminal justice.

CRIME AS THE VIOLATION OF HUMAN RIGHTS

The key proponents of this argument are Herman and Julia Schwendinger (1970).

Their approach argues that all humans have certain natural rights, such as, right to life, liberty, good health, freedom of movement, happiness, etc. According to this perspective, criminology should be the study of the violation of human rights. This, they argue, provides a more objective unit of study than that provided by the legalistic position on crime. This perspective also allows for states and governments to be judged to be criminal. They asked:

> Isn't it time to raise serious questions about the assumptions underlying the definition of the field of criminology, when a man who steals a paltry sum can be called a criminal while agents of the State can, with impunity, legally reward men who destroy food so that price levels can be maintained whilst a sizable portion of the population suffers from malnutrition? (Schwendinger and Schwendinger, 1970: 137)

However, this approach does not solve all problems regarding definitions. Do people all around the world agree on what human rights people are entitled to? Is there a consensus on what constitutes a right? Their argument requires people to accept that a consensus can be reached.

CRIME AS A SOCIAL CONSTRUCTION

The concept of crime as a social construction is one that suggests that crime is decided by society. Society makes the laws that regulate individuals' behaviour, and so society determines what is considered criminal and what is lawful.

Those who see crime as a social construction suggest that deviance 'is in the eyes of the beholder'. In other words, there is nothing inherently criminal about a certain act. Therefore it would follow that the focus of criminology should be how and why some acts become criminal and others do not. The vital questions for those who see crime as a social construction is, 'in whose interest was it that a certain act was criminalized?'

The most frequently cited work of relevance that argues that crime is a social construction is that of Howard Becker, who argued that 'social groups create deviance by making the rules whose infraction constitutes deviance' (Becker, 1963: 8). This is one of the most used quotes in criminology.

More recently the socially constructed nature of crime is recognised, for example, by those of a cultural criminological persuasion. Similarly, those of a critical persuasion continue to highlight how the contemporary social construction of crime often locates the most serious crimes at the bottom of the social strata, while failing to see the 'criminality' of expense-swindling politicians, corporate crooks, reckless bankers, profit-chasing entrepreneurs whose behaviour may be little formally criminalized. Indeed, while this may be changing in the wake of the global financial crisis, it remains a most pertinent point that the legal status of a behaviour – and whether that behaviour is defined as a crime – lies not in the content of the behaviour itself but in the social responses to and the social and moral standing of the offenders and the victims.

In criminology it is important that the use of the terms 'crime' and 'criminal' must be carefully considered. Who and what is considered criminal is a complex debate without easy answers. If you understand this you have moved away from commonsense and opinion-based arguments about crime to a point where you think more carefully. In doing this you are beginning to think like a criminologist!

1.7   CATEGORISING CRIMINOLOGICAL THEORY

In reading Part 2 of this book you will be exposed to a wide array of criminological theory and theorists. It is at this point, however, that I advise you to read this part with caution, and to bear in mind that the terms we use to make sense of different theories will vary. So, for example, one theory may be known by a number of different names. In addition, some criminologists over time have aligned themselves with various different theoretical perspectives.

You should also be careful to try to avoid associating criminologists with specific theories. It is always worth remembering the words of one of Britain's most prominent criminologists, Sir Leon Radzinowicz, who suggested that 'the tendency amongst a number of criminologists to attach labels to each other is rather widespread, though by no means always fair or correct' (Radzinowicz, 1999: 198). Try to look at criminological writing with an open mind and see how theory is used in it, but don't assume that the author necessarily subscribes to a specific theoretical position.

PART TWO
CORE AREAS OF THE CURRICULUM

RUNNING THEMES IN CRIMINOLOGY

Throughout this book, you will be asked to consider running themes. These are some of the issues and considerations that underpin the discipline of criminology, and have to be considered regardless of the topic. You are encouraged to re-visit the running themes continually, and reflect upon the subject matter with these in mind, asking questions about how each theme may impact upon individual subject areas.

RUNNING THEMES

No matter what area of criminology you are writing about, it is important that you try, wherever possible, to mention these themes and think about how they make an impact upon the subject:

- **Inequality** – Who loses and who gains in a social context? Is something fair, and are people regarded equally? If not there may be inequality.
- **Power** – Who defines the agenda, and how do they use force, ideas, language, etc. to control behaviour?
- **Evidence** – How convincing is an argument? What basis does the argument have? Little is ever proven, and there will be a counter argument. What is it?
- **Class** – How does our social background affect our opportunities, our choices, and our identity?
- **Discrimination** – Is one group, or groups, disproportionately advantaged or disadvantaged? Are some people being treated markedly differently to the advantage or disadvantage of others?
- **Sex and gender** – How does being male or female differ in a given social context, and how does the social context shape our options as women or as men?

- **Race** – How does ethnicity make a difference? Some people may face prejudice and inequality because of their ethnicity and culture.
- **Research methods** – How have the methods used to generate social observations made those observations any more or any less convincing to you? You should also consider what the research is based upon. Is the research based upon evidence, and what is the evidence? How does the research base support any claims being made?
- **Age** – Whether you are old or young, a child or a grown-up, you will experience social life differently and may have different opportunities.
- **Ideology** – What are the tacit rules and regulations that govern how we think about every social problem, and what is it that stops us thinking differently?
- **Politics/economics** – How do either the politics and/or economics of the issue limit choice and govern social action?
- **Application** – Theories may have a practical purpose. What are, or might be, the practical implications of a theory?
- **Representation** – What picture is being portrayed? What is being suggested, and by what/whom?
- **Justice** – This has a variety of applications, but most literally could be taken as incorporating the notion of fairness and appropriateness in the exercise of authority. Is a concept fair? Does it treat the subject appropriately? This, however, is a subjective concept. It is not fixed or universal, but based upon individual opinion and judgement.

USING RUNNING THEMES

When writing about crime you will need to talk about how crime is not a simple concept. You could argue that crime is not something we can all define, and you may argue that who defines crime is a matter of power. You could suggest that crime reflects inequality in terms of those who experience it – the experience of crime (and the perpetration of crime) differs according to whether you are working class or middle class, male or female, black or white, young or old. You will also need to remember, as is suggested below, that the nature and experience of crime is always changing, as are the methods we use both to record it and to control it. Already, in a short space of time you have begun to interweave some of the running themes listed above. Without naming a particular study or theorist, you have already set out a strong structure to any argument, and you are showing that you can think like a criminologist.

2.1   THE ORIGINS OF CRIMINOLOGY

CORE AREAS

The contested origins of criminology

Spiritual explanations

A capital system

The background to the development of criminology

Cesare Beccaria – The philanthropist?

Beccaria – *On Crimes and Punishments*

Criticisms of classicism

RUNNING THEMES

Classical criminology was based on arguments about the cause of crime and how it should be dealt with. It had no concern with **research methods** as it was not based upon **evidence**, but instead on arguments about the **ideology** of crime and punishment. Therefore, classical criminology is inspired by **political** and **economic** thought. That stated, the motivations that influenced this school of criminology are not clear. Some criminologists would argue that classicism served to challenge **inequality** and inappropriate use of **power**, while others feel that it is **class** biased, and its central motivation was to continue to promote **inequalities** and the authority and **power** of the social elite.

KEY THINKERS

Cesare Beccaria (1738–94) Cesare Bonesana, Marchese de Beccaria (more frequently referred to as Cesare Beccaria) was born to a respected aristocratic family in Milan, Italy. Beccaria was a philosopher with an interest in economics. Through a friendship with Alessandro Verri (who was at the time the Protector for Prisoners) he was persuaded to write on the topic of crime and punishment. Initially, he published his work *Dei Deliti e Delle Pene* [*On Crimes and Punishments*] in 1764 anonymously, through fear as to how it would be received. His fear was ill-founded and Beccaria eventually came to be much respected.

Jeremy Bentham (1748–1832) Bentham was a British Jurist and philosopher who is associated with the concept of utilitarianism. His contribution to criminology is varied and includes the design of the Panopticon prison, a model that was to influence much Victorian prison building.

THE CONTESTED ORIGINS OF CRIMINOLOGY

The origins of criminology as an academic discipline are contested, but most criminology courses and textbooks will begin by examining the contribution of a school of thought called 'classicism' or 'classical criminology'. This is by no means universally accepted as the origin of criminology, because for some criminologists it is not possible to regard what was essentially a philosophical strand of thought as the origin of criminology.

It is also worth stressing at this point that classicism may be a concept that is perhaps used more for academics' convenience than because of the existence of a unified 'classical school' of criminology. In creating a category of classical criminology, textbook histories often conform to one of two styles. The first style highlights one or two prominent names, giving rise to the false idea that these stand out as isolated contributors. The second convention paints a no more accurate picture, and tends to bring together a range of contributors to early criminology that could only be linked very tenuously.

Part of the problem is that there does not exist an identifiable starting point for criminology as a subject; it is not possible to find a logical or decisive moment in which 'criminology' was created (in just the same way as it is not possible to suggest a universal rule that explains all crime). There is a great deal of merit in studying early contributions to debates about the causation of crime, because if you can understand this background, you are probably better placed to understand contemporary criminology.

SPIRITUAL EXPLANATIONS

Spiritual explanations for crime form part of a general view of life in which events are linked to a higher power, or the influence of otherworldly powers.

Primitive people believed natural events such as earthquakes, famines and floods were punishments sent by spiritual powers or gods (divine retribution) to punish wrong-doing. In the Middle Ages this spirituality became linked to political systems, with society structured around monarchy and aristocracy creating feudal systems to which we can trace the origins of our criminal justice system. In these systems, crime was often avenged or dealt with between family groups and allegiance, or by those with power. The taking of blood oaths of vengeance by victims was common, and the principles regarding punishment often involved exacting justice by revisiting harm proportionate or greater than that done initially, back upon the offender (an eye for an eye).

Feudal justice systems were based upon rights of power whereby 'God's will' would see justice done. Examples of this are trial by battle whereby two opposing parties (or their representatives) would fight in combat with God giving victory to the winner; the loser would then have no grounds for attempting to exact revenge. Trial by ordeal was introduced somewhat later (an example being trial by fire where holding or walking on burning coals was used to determine guilt). In western European systems the link between law and monarchy was one that continued in most countries until modern times. That said, the method for punishing wrong-doing was often crude, and progressed little from cruel vengeance.

A CAPITAL SYSTEM

From the fifth century in Anglo-Saxon England, when execution by 'hanging' emerged as the dominant form of punishment for many offences (it was applied with alarming frequency until around the end of the 1850s), the methods for delivering punishment were often cruel and gruesome. In England, women charged with 'petty treason' (killing their spouse) were covered in tar and burnt at the stake in public until 1789. Punishments often made little allowances for mitigation. In 1708, Michael Hammond (then aged 7) and his sister (aged 11) were reputedly hanged for felony offences – if true, Michael would have been the youngest person ever to suffer the death penalty in Britain. Even in the nineteenth century capital punishment was a sentence that was applicable to a vast range of crimes (in 1822 English and Welsh law listed a staggering 222 capital criminal offences). Gradually the use of transportation to America (and later Australia) allowed for death sentences to be commuted to transportation, and there was a shift in the nature of punishment from corporal punishment to imprisonment. However, it is largely execution and savage retribution and injustice that form the backdrop to the emergence of classical criminology.

Even with the Penitentiary Act, the first English legislation authorising state run-prisons, which was passed in 1779, punishment was often a violent and painful experience.

THE BACKGROUND TO THE DEVELOPMENT OF CRIMINOLOGY

The majority of criminological textbooks tend to begin their accounts in the mid-eighteenth century. Indeed it is easy to see why criminology's origins are linked to this time. Britain provides illustration of the way writings on the subject of law, crime and criminals became increasingly visible.

In 1756, William Blackstone published his lectures; a conservative appraisal of 'the *Development of the Laws of England*' suggested that the development of the law embodied the collective wisdom of society. It was in criticism of this notion that Bentham published a critical response and set the foundations for the principles of unity (and the concept of utilitarianism) in 1776. Utilitarianism is a concept that is often associated with classical criminology.

Utilitarianism
As a concept, utilitarianism stems from the work of Jeremy Bentham and John Stuart Mill. It is a moral theory that asserts that what is good is that which seeks to minimize pain, but maximize pleasure. The other core principle of utilitarianism is that the aim of good law should be to promote the greatest happiness for the greatest number.

CESARE BECCARIA – THE PHILANTHROPIST?

Many books on criminology will link the origins of criminology to Cesare Beccaria. As an Italian aristocrat, Beccaria was able to turn his attention to philosophical debates on crime. It has to be remembered that the society in which he existed was far different to that which exists today. Western European states were largely governed by monarchy, with the monarch and the state assuming moral responsibility to impose punishment on offenders (in effect, assuming the authority of God and claiming a divine power to impose punishment on offenders).

These punishments, as illustrated above, were often cruel and harsh, based upon the infliction of pain and suffering. Many countries used the death penalty excessively for a wide range of offences. With severe and barbaric punishments commonplace, torture rife, and capricious judges interpreting the law often on a whim (or adding punishments for personal reasons), the system of law was perhaps ripe for reform. A number of criminological textbooks regard 'classicism' as an example of enlightened humanitarian thinking. Beccaria's work is often regarded as an example of 'enlightenment' thinking that emerged in the late eighteenth century as a challenge to the dominance of spiritual and religious ideas.

Of course an alternative view exists, which suggests that the increasing concern with the welfare of offenders must be considered in the context of a more general shift in western European states. These societies were beginning to move towards an industrial phase, and the ruling class could ill afford to damage or destroy the bodies of the labouring classes any longer. For that reason, it has been suggested that punishment of the body was being replaced by 'control' over it (a concept that stems from the seminal work of Michel Foucault, 1977).

The concern of the ruling classes about their privilege and its potential to be challenged might also provide a motivation for classicism. It is worth noting that when Beccaria published *On Crimes and Punishments* in 1764, the world was entering a period characterized by challenges to monarchy and the authority of states. The American Revolution occurred just over a decade later (in 1776), followed by the French Revolution (in 1789). Both displayed a lack of will to accept as given the power of rulers, which would have concerned the social elite throughout Europe. Therefore any analysis of 'classicism' or classical criminology should consider the perceived threat to the power of the dominant class and how this might have served to motivate them to create more humane regimes, rather than regard the motivation simply with a humane concern for promoting justice.

BECCARIA – *ON CRIMES AND PUNISHMENTS*

On Crimes and Punishments was essentially a challenge to the Italian state's existing criminal justice systems. Beccaria protested against the inconsistencies in government and the management of public affairs. A particular point of contention for him was what he perceived to be purely personal justice that was being administered by judges. Beccaria's arguments are well documented; however, they are essentially philosophical rather than based upon research evidence, and were clearly based upon value judgements that he made.

Cesare Beccaria's *On Crimes and Punishments* (1764)

- Men give up, or sacrifice a proportion of their liberty so as to enjoy the rest of it in peace and security. The sum of those portions is what makes up the sovereignty of a nation.
- But this alone is not enough, because these portions must be defended against individuals who may attempt to usurp a greater share. Some people will try not only to withdraw *their* share, but that of others. Tangible motives are needed to prevent this, and these motives are punishments established against those who may break the law.
- The despotic spirit and the propensity to commit crime exists within all people.
- Punishment should be dictated by legislation, and not decided by the courts.
- Punishment that exceeds that limit fixed in law is not just punishment. The law should set punishments, and it should not be possible for judges to go beyond the limits set in law.
- The true measure of crime is not the harm done to society, but the harm the criminal intended to do.
- There must be a proper proportion between crimes and punishments (the punishment should fit the crime).
- Punishment is effective when the damage that it does exceeds the advantage gained from the crime.
- The more promptly the punishment follows the crime, the more just and useful it is.
- One of the most effective curbs on crimes is not the severity of the punishment, but the certainty that punishment will follow crime.
- The laws must be clear and simple, so everyone may understand them.
- Activities not expressly prohibited by law are permissible.
- As punishment was to be imposed for deterrence, capital punishment for the most part should be abolished.
- Classicism formed the basis for the French penal code of 1791, and some of the core principles of classicism can still be seen in the administration of justice to this day.

CRITICISMS OF CLASSICISM

There are problems with the classical position – for example, the assumption of free will could be argued to be flawed. The idea that criminals are fundamentally rational and offend due to a desire for pleasure is one that will never gain universal acceptance. Such views tend to regard those who offend as having a choice, but there are other reasons why people offend, and not all people have the same options or choices available to them. This view does not take into consideration the inequality of opportunities in society, which is perhaps unsurprising when one considers the background of those who generated it.

- Classicism assumes that people weigh up the costs and benefits of their crimes before they commit them – this may be true for some criminals, but it is not the case for all. We know that many crimes are spontaneous and ill considered.
- Classicism assumes that people are knowledgeable about the punishments for crimes but again, this is often not the case, as many people do not know what the punishment for a specific offence is.
- Classicism argues for treating all people as alike – therefore the first-time offender commits an act as grave as the serial recidivist; the young and the mentally ill are equally culpable; first-time offenders are treated in the same way as repeat offenders.
- The idea that everyone suffers the same punishment in the same way may be naïve. People have different responses to punishment. We know that for some offenders prison is a terrible experience, while others might suggest that they find it comforting and familiar.
- Judging the seriousness of a crime on the basis of act alone, and not intention, is also problematic. This view would see a 'cold blooded' and premeditated murder the same as an accidental or involuntary homicide. The harm resultant is the same: someone dies – yet the intent is markedly different. Classicism suggests no distinction need be made.
- Classicism advocates a universal acceptance of the law simply because it is law, and does not question whether such laws are fair or just. It does not take into account the fact that societies are inherently unfair. For some people the cost of adhering to the social contract is nothing, and yet they gain a great deal of protection (especially those who are privileged and have a lot to lose). For others the costs are great and the benefits few. If we accept that this is the case, then increasing the benefits of adhering to the social contract may be more effective than having punishment for those who breach it. This, however, was not an attractive option to some social contract theorists who tended to come from a particular status group within society.

If you want to write about classicism, you would be well advised to consider the 'Running themes' such as those of inequality, power and class. How does classicism acknowledge these issues? Also, what is its research base and research methodology? How effective and useful would you evaluate classicism as being? Consider this using the Running themes and criteria for evaluating theory given in Chapter 3.2.

'What were the factors that influenced the development of classical criminology?'

Too many students fail to adequately address the fact that there are a wide range of criminologists who can be associated with the classical tradition. A good answer will identify some of the features of classical criminology, and make a well-rounded argument about its development. Remember that there are two perspectives you can take: one holds that classicism was inspired by humanitarian concerns; the other that it was the product of a ruling class keen to protect its property. You should try to decide which you feel is more convincing and why. Remember to mention some specific theorists and their works.

Further resources

I would encourage students to develop a more insightful view of the origins of criminology than most textbooks provide. Although it is complex and somewhat dated, Wayne Morrison's book *Theoretical Criminology* (1995) is still worth reading. Steve Hall's (2012) *Theorising Crime and Deviance: A New Perspective* which is a challenging but rewarding, critique of the philosophical and political underpinnings of criminological theory, and also provides a useful account of the development of theoretical criminology over the twentieth century.

Excerpts of both Beccaria's and Bentham's works appear in McLaughlin et al.'s book *Criminological Perspectives* (2003). At the beginning of any criminology course I would encourage students to purchase a copy of *The Sage Dictionary of Criminology* (McLaughlin and Muncie, 2001) which may prove difficult reading at first, but ultimately is an invaluable resource to students new to the discipline.

2.2   RESEARCH METHODS IN CRIMINOLOGY

CORE AREAS

Research in criminology

Primary and secondary research

Quantitative research methods

Qualitative research methods

Combined methods

Epistemology: Positivist, interpretivist and critical

Ethics

Access

The politics of criminological research

RUNNING THEMES

Questions about research and its **evidence** base will underpin almost all considerations of criminological theory. What is it that leads a criminologist to his/her conclusions? What do they base their assertions on? In many cases, research in criminology will be based upon empirical work, and therefore we need to understand and ask questions about the **research methods** being used if we are to determine whether the picture being presented is a fair **representation**. It should be remembered that the research process is one that involves **power**, and can be influenced by eternal factors such as **politics** and **economics**.

RESEARCH IN CRIMINOLOGY

In order to develop an understanding of criminology it is vital that you have some knowledge about the practice of generating 'empirical' research on crime and criminal justice. Criminologists seek to prove or support theories with evidence; often relying upon empirical evidence (which means evidence based upon observation and experiment and not just theory alone).

Not all criminological research is empirical; there is a wealth of criminological research that is purely 'theoretical', and this does not necessarily make that work invalid. In criminology the two have to co-exist, so empirical research is used to make theoretical arguments, or generate concepts that will become theories. Alternatively, having a theory, idea or hypothesis may be the starting point for conducting empirical research.

> As a criminologist it is important that you can comment on whether research is good or not, and in order to do this you have to be able to evaluate theories. (This is covered in more detail in Part 3.)

> By 'empirical' we mean research that is based upon knowledge that has been generated by observation and experiment, rather than simply upon theory.

PRIMARY AND SECONDARY RESEARCH

As a social science, criminology has two types of data that may be used in the research process. The first, or 'primary', data to the social scientist is data that they themselves have collected. A variety of different research methods may have been used to collect this data (for example interviews, questionnaires and observations). A 'secondary' source is information that has been produced by someone else, but a social scientist uses it for his or her own purposes.

Primary and secondary data

- Primary methods – these involve data collection methods such as observation, questionnaires, structured and semi-structured interviews, focus groups, and participant observations.
- Secondary methods – these involve re-analysing official crime statistics and using existing literature, information obtained from previous research, or from someone else.

QUANTITATIVE RESEARCH METHODS

Most criminologists need theory to be supported by some form of 'empirical' evidence gained from research, and therefore will actively undertake research. When they do this they will tend to draw upon one tradition in research.

There are essentially two traditional research methods in criminological research, the first, what we call the quantitative tradition, emerged with the early positivists and moral statisticians, who proposed that it was possible to study society scientifically. The second is the qualitative tradition, which we will look at in more detail below.

Researchers who adhere to a quantitative approach are concerned with explaining crime and predicting future patterns of criminal behaviour. Early positivists were keen to move away from simply philosophical discussions about crime and instead study society and social phenomena by drawing upon methods and ideas associated with the natural sciences. They were concerned with developing knowledge about the 'causation' of human behaviour, including criminal behaviour, which could be presented in the form of rules or laws.

Clearly, if causes could be found, then so might cures, and therefore much early positivistic criminology (such as the work of Lombroso) was thought to be potentially useful. Often positivists start with a hypothesis (that is, an idea or concept) that they will then seek to prove or disprove by testing, much like in the natural sciences.

Quantitative work continues to be undertaken in criminology, and much of the research that is produced by government departments is quantitative in nature. It is perhaps important to state here, though, that there has been a distinct shift in much quantitative work in criminology. The zealous search for a 'cause' of crime is no longer the driving force behind most criminology, and criminologists do not often seek to put forward a causal explanation for all crime. Quantitative researchers no longer conform to the narrow positivistic traditions that early criminologists did. Instead they tend to focus on a vast array of factors that may influence trends in crime or criminal behaviour.

QUALITATIVE RESEARCH METHODS

This approach was developed in the Chicago School of Sociology in the United States in the 1920s and 1930s. Much of the product of the Chicago School's research was concerned with the study of the sociology of deviance, and relied upon ethnographic methods.

Ethnography is the study of people and groups in their natural setting, typically involving the researcher spending prolonged periods of time systematically gathering data about their day-to-day activities, and the meanings that are attached to them.

Qualitative research rejects the notion that society and social phenomena can be studied in the same way as natural phenomena. Included in the Chicago School's ethnographies were studies of homelessness, prostitution and delinquent gangs. These theories gained followers and influence, where they continued to provide rich insight into the subculture of deviant groups (perhaps best known is Becker's 1963 study of cannabis use titled *Outsiders*). By the 1950s this approach had started to influence British sociologists producing studies of youth delinquency (Mays, 1954; Downes, 1966). More recently, qualitative research has been increasingly accepted by academics, and has been used to study a variety of topics in criminology. It has also been extremely influential upon those who now term themselves 'cultural criminologists'. It is generally accepted that qualitative research can offer rich insights into people's attitudes, beliefs and values and therefore is extremely useful to criminologists.

COMBINED METHODS

Whilst you could now be forgiven for believing that quantitative and qualitative methods are opposed, caution is advised and we must be mindful not to be drawn into thinking that the distinctions between the two are always immediately apparent. While it is true to suggest that some researchers divide the two methods (and themselves) into distinct camps from where they can be very critical of the opposition, many researchers tend to use methods combining quantitative and qualitative analysis (sometimes in the same research study). This is done in order that they use a robust and defensible methodology, and to pre-empt and counter potential criticisms.

EPISTEMOLOGY: POSITIVE, INTERPRETIVIST AND CRITICAL

Social scientific researchers are not only influenced by research methods, but also by ideas about how knowledge is generated. To describe this we use the word 'epistemology', which literally means theories of knowledge. The term 'epistemology' describes a researcher's beliefs about the nature of the social world that is under study, and the assumptions made about how we should generate knowledge.

> Regardless of the methods that researchers use, there are different 'epistemological' positions that they will occupy, that may (but will not necessarily) influence their selected research methods.

In criminology there exist different theories of knowledge, which we term 'epistemologies'. These flow from the early philosophical debates in the social sciences.

Positivist
The first epistemology is the 'positivist' approach, or positivism, which is now widely considered amongst social scientists to be an outdated view.

Those who subscribe to a positivist epistemology believe that it is possible to be value-neutral when conducting research, and that by being value-neutral, the research is objective and not influenced by the researchers' own values or opinions. The main concern with this approach is the discovery of causal factors and relationships (for example, does a lack of street lighting cause a higher level of crime?). As an approach it is often linked with quantitative research, generating a hypothesis or idea such as the previous example, which is then subjected to testing.

Interpretivist

The interpretivist approach rejects the concept that science and scientific method can be used to study the thoughts and feelings that impact upon human behaviour and interactions, and posits that the only way that researchers generate ideas is by interpreting what they encounter. Clearly such a belief immediately lends itself more readily to qualitative research approaches. Unlike the positivist epistemology, it doesn't claim to be value-neutral, so it is therefore regarded as much more subjective and opinion-based.

Critical

Critical epistemology (or critical social research epistemology) aims to challenge both the positivist and interpretivist epistemologies. It does not necessarily avoid science, or claims to be scientific, but neither does it claim to be a value-neutral process. Instead, critical social researchers would assert that all research is underpinned by values. It will also not necessarily avoid interpretation, instead it intends to locate itself within a more balanced position. Critical social research believes that research should reveal the processes through which dominant understandings of the world are constructed. As an approach it promotes the use of a variety of research methods, believing that what is most important is that the methods selected are the most appropriate to the issue that is being studied. Critical social research attempts to shed light upon the way in which the dominant ideas and understanding of the world are created and maintained. It regards all knowledge as socially produced. The critical epistemology attempts to 'see the bigger picture'.

All too often in criminological research there is a tendency to simply promote one method (quantitative or qualitative) and criticize the other. Too often it could be believed that there exist only two epistemological traditions (positivism and interpretivism) with academics attaching themselves to one tradition and attacking the other.

Table 2.1 Epistemologies

	Positivism	Interpretivism	Critical
Assumptions about the nature of the social world that is under study	• There is an 'objective external reality' that can be discovered by research	• There is no 'objective reality' because we construct reality in a social context. What counts as 'real' are those things that we are conscious of	• Accepts that reality is constructed, but in different ways, and at different times, and different places. However, this does not mean that these constructions do not have real effects upon people. Some constructions become dominant and inform the way our society is structured. We have to understand the ways and processes in which we come to understand the world. We need to consider how society is structured and in whose interest. Research needs to make inequalities visible and challenge 'common sense'
Epistemological assumptions – that is, assumptions about how we should generate knowledge	• Knowledge of the social world should be gained in the same way that scientists gain knowledge of the natural world. It should be based upon the collection of 'fact' and through the testing of hypothesis	• The social world is completely different to the natural world; and we cannot treat people as objects. Therefore knowledge must be gained via interpretation – what meaning do people attach to their experiences?	
Preference in terms of research methodology	• Key concepts: explanation, objectivity	• Key concepts: interpretation, meaning, subjectivity	• Key concepts: theoretical understanding; objectivity (but that doesn't mean value freedom – we all have values)
	• Quantitative methods and hypothesis testing	• Qualitative methods	• Methods are selected according to the question

ETHICS

Ethical concerns in research are about the principles that inform our research practices. Social scientists use the term 'ethics' to describe and debate what we deem appropriate and inappropriate during the research process. Such concerns have always played a major part in all forms of social research. It is difficult to talk generally about ethics, because what is ethical and what is not will depend to some extent upon individual values, attitudes and beliefs (that stated, while we will all have different opinions on matters involving ethics, we have an obligation to consider the ethical implications of our work).

There is a general consensus amongst criminologists, for example, regarding the fact that anonymity should be afforded to informants, and consent should be sought wherever possible. This openness (sometimes described as overt research) may still vary because even if researchers are overt and open about the research, how much detail informants give will vary. As criminological research often involves some degree of risk (for example, the researcher may not be granted permission or consent of those people or organizations they wish to study, or may face a combination of both of these considerations), some criminologists choose the opposite approach (that is, covert research). Covert research is secretive, and participants will not be aware that they are being observed, and in some cases the researcher may even go so far as to deliberately deceive or lie in order to keep the research secretive. Clearly the methodology will be somewhat dependent upon the 'ethical' principles to which individual or groups of researchers subscribe, and the validity of each method is an ethical judgement that only the researcher can make.

When we consider research (whether conducting it or commenting upon it) it is important that we take account of not only what the research tells us, but also the ethics that informed the study and potential ethical dilemmas that the findings of the research might raise.

ACCESS

Access is a term that we use in criminology to describe gaining permission or admittance to conduct study. This might sound simple but we should not forget that in almost all research, access will be a recurring theme, for example, each time you meet potential informants you will have to renegotiate access. Gaining access can involve approaching an individual (e.g. a prison governor) or a group (e.g. prison officers) or an agency (e.g. the prison service more generally). Access may also involve documents (e.g. pre-sentence reports). In criminological research access can be one of the most important considerations – we must ask questions about access, who gains access to conduct research, and more importantly, how and why?

THE POLITICS OF CRIMINOLOGICAL RESEARCH

It is important to remember that research does not take place in a void, and that there will be a vast number of factors that will influence research processes. Just as the criminal justice system will be linked to a vast amount of political and ideological arguments, so will research. The challenge that 'critical' and 'interpretivist' epistemologies have made to the notion of value-freedom in social research has been very significant. There are few social scientists who continue to argue that when research is produced it should be wholly value-neutral, and most criminologists will now acknowledge (some happily, some more reluctantly) that their research is not value-free.

Criminologists must be aware that the research they undertake can potentially have an impact upon both criminal justice policy and practices, for better and for worse! In criminological research there are essentially a number of areas where political considerations may be of influence and the following should be remembered.

In researching crime and deviance, criminologists are dealing with subject matter that is commonly regarded as socially problematic, and therefore it is something that is likely to be subject to political discussion, policy and initiateves. Criminological researchers are also involved in numerous political processes on a smaller scale because research often seeks to understand the standpoints of differing, sometimes oppositional groups, regardless of whether one subscribes to the concept of value–neutrality or not.

'What are the strengths of quantitative and qualitative research? Can you think of a research project that would be best suited to i) qualitative methods, ii) quantitative methods, iii) both quantitative and qualitative methods?'

When addressing this type of question you should clearly demonstrate knowledge of the differences between each research approach, and be able to identify where each is suitable. You should also remember that increasingly, criminologists are combining methods to generate the most accurate research possible. Remember that using examples from recent research projects will almost always be beneficial. Remember that qualitative and quantitative methods lend themselves to different tasks, and you can illustrate this with examples.

Further resources

Examples of current research (both quantitative and qualitative) can be accessed through the Home Office website (see http://www.homeoffice.gov.uk/science-research/science-publications/). Look at some examples and ask yourself whether the research supports the assertions that the criminologist in question is making. What might be the benefit/drawback of their methodology? Also think in some detail about what the researcher has said. What might have led to their conclusions? Will the conclusions be based solely upon research evidence generated, upon the researcher's personal beliefs and values, or might economic/political factors have played a part?

There are numerous good books and chapters in books on the subject of criminological research. Students should see Pam Davies et al. (2010) *Doing Criminological Research* as an excellent introduction. David Gadd et al. (2010) *The Sage Handbook of Criminological Research Methods* brings together a large group of experienced researchers from across the globe to cover a wide range of innovative and important approaches to criminological enquiry. Finally, Westmarland (2011) *Researching Crime and Justice: Tales from the Field* is an interesting engagement with criminologists who have used various methods and would provide an excellent source of additional reading for those new to the social sciences.

2.3   LOCATING CRIME WITHIN THE INDIVIDUAL: BIOLOGICAL AND PSYCHOLOGICAL APPROACHES

CORE AREAS

Early positivism in criminology

Early criminology inspired by positivism

Early biological criminology

Psychological theories

Why are biological and psychological theories influential?

RUNNING THEMES

Biological and psychological approaches to criminology have searched for causes of crime. The **research methods** that inform such studies and the **evidence** that they present must be examined carefully. Biological and psychological criminology can present persuasive arguments, but they can also contain very **discriminatory** ideas about issues such as **race**, **sex** and **gender** that could lead to **inequality**. We therefore also have to question what the **practical application** of these theories may be.

Common pitfall

A problem that arises in criminology when we create categories and terms is that they are not fixed or universally agreed upon (although some textbooks suggest they are). This can often cause confusion when two criminologists use different terms to describe what is actually the same theory.

Remember that whilst psychological, sociological and biological theories are often separated in textbooks, the real world and real crime probably need to acknowledge elements of each. Psychological theories and biological theories need not ignore sociological factors.

It will help you if from the outset you do not worry too much about categories, but pay attention to the core elements of theories. This involves asking what the theory is concerned with. If we think just about categories we notice that psychological criminological theories tend to place emphasis upon factors such as emotional adjustment and personality, while sociological criminology is more likely to be concerned instead with, say, cultural values and status. Problems arise when these theories become mixed together, and this happens frequently.

EARLY POSITIVISM IN CRIMINOLOGY

The decline of classicism can essentially be seen as mirroring the rise of a positivist criminology that claimed to promote the scientific study of society, and replace philosophical judgement and opinion with empirically grounded fact and science. Many criminological textbooks tell a conventional tale of an emerging new, scientific positivistic criminology banishing the philosophical thinking that preceded it, only to turn and ridicule this positivism in the next paragraph.

If you were to read many of the accounts of the emergence of biological positivism, this is what you might well expect to encounter. The reality, however, is not so stark, and the distance that we have travelled from the frequently ridiculed biological positivism of Lombroso (and certainly psychological positivism) may not be so far as we would like to think. In reality it is difficult in many ways to see any real decline in the principal arguments of classical and early positivist criminology. Consider for a minute the opinions you have heard expressed on the subject of crime. I am certain that 'choice' or 'free will' would be familiar concepts, as may a lack of choice. As a counter to this, positivism held that for some people there may be factors that propelled them toward crime. Positivism in criminology sought to explain and predict future patterns of social behaviour, using secondary statistical data, and later, methods linked with knowledge of medicine, psychiatry and psychology. It tends to be associated with the scientific commitment to finding facts on the causes of crime. Positivistic research forms the basic methodology for a vast array of criminological research that is undertaken in accordance with positivistic principles, such as deductive reasoning, striving for value-neutrality in research, generating and testing hypotheses through measurement, and ensuring that research is objective.

> Positivism is a research method and not a specific branch of criminology! Positivism spans biological, psychological and sociological attempts to identify key causes of crime. These are then often presented as 'causal factors' of crime, largely regarded as outside the individual's control. Therefore positivism can tend to regard criminality as predetermined rather than chosen. It is often seen as contrasting with many of the arguments made by the classical school of criminology. Indeed, much contemporary criminology is still an epistemology (or collection of epistemologies) with an empiricism that is opposed to realism. Much contemporary quantitative criminology could still be said to be positivistic. The table below contrasts the core principles of positivism and classicism.

Table 2.2

Classicism	Positivism
Humans are rational beings and their actions can be understood as 'free will'	Human actions are, to a large extent, determined by forces beyond an individual's control
Crime can be regarded as an error of rational judgement or a mistake	Individuals are propelled towards crime by biological, sociological and psychological factors over which they have little control
Punishment can act as a deterrent	Treatment can assist in preventing further offending
The punishment should fit the offence	Treatment should be tailored to fit the specific needs of the offender

EARLY CRIMINOLOGY INSPIRED BY POSITIVISM

KEY THINKER

Cesare Lombroso (1836–1909) The founder of the 'Italian Positivist School', Lombroso was a medical physician whose major work *L'Uomo Delinquente* [*The Criminal Man*] was first published in 1876. Lombroso put forward the idea (based on research on offenders) that there were different types of criminal, including the 'born criminal' who was a throwback to an earlier stage of evolution, and was therefore socially inferior to normal people. Lombroso termed this 'atavism' and suggested that there were atavistic stigma present on the bodies of criminals which could be identified and measured. He was heavily influenced by positivism in terms of his methodology, producing what is termed 'anthropometric research' (which describes attempts to derive character traits by measuring features of the body) that was quantitative in nature.

EARLY BIOLOGICAL CRIMINOLOGY

Many criminological textbooks acknowledge Lombroso as the founder of criminology, which is interesting given that at the time of Lombroso's writing he was only one of a group of professionals and interested parties who had turned their attentions to the study of the criminal (admittedly many did not claim to adopt the scientific rigour that Lombroso suggested of his work).

The growth of imprisonment as a punishment had supplied prison surgeons with subjects to observe. In *Criminal Sociology*, published in 1895, Ferri (one of Lombroso's students) mentions a number of works generated prior to Lombroso's publication of *The Criminal Man*. These observations were also not restricted to studies of the body. In *The Descent of Man*, Charles Darwin noted the influence of psychologist Dr Prosper Despine, who, as early as 1868, gave 'many curious cases of the worst criminals, who apparently have been entirely destitute of conscience' (1885: 78). Many of the very first explanations of criminal and deviant behaviour were biological, and certainly, much early criminological research was positivistic in its method and the preserve of the medically trained and educated classes.

> Remember that positivism is a research method and not a distinct strand of criminological thought. Therefore you should perhaps try, where possible, to avoid talking about 'positivist criminology' in a general sense. Can the work of Lombroso really be compared to, say, a study of street lighting on a council estate in the 1980s that uses a positivistic methodology?

While Lombroso's work could be placed under the heading of biological criminology, investigations of the causes of criminality using more sophisticated research methods examining biological criminological theories have continued to be developed in the twentieth century. These have examined:

- intelligence (suggesting that offenders mostly have a low IQ)
- genetic abnormalities
- hyper-masculinity and the aggressive male
- the influence of testosterone (a hormone that can increase aggression)
- adrenaline (another hormone)
- neurotransmitters (substances like serotonin and dopamine that transmit signals between neurons and the brain)
- heredity and potential transfer of criminal tendencies (by studying twins and those who have been adopted)
- factors related to nutrition (such as blood sugar levels, vitamins and minerals) and any potential influence on levels of criminality.

All of these have a biological component and all are based upon 'scientific' research. Much as Lombroso searched for physical causes of crime, these studies have shared that concern. Yet whilst biological explanations may explain why some individuals do commit crime, they can never explain all criminal behaviour. (However, some researchers confidently suggest they have – for example, criminologist Johannes Lange (1931) was convinced criminality was inherited from parents, and he titled his book *Crime as Destiny*).

The weaknesses of biological explanations can be offset somewhat if criminologists and researchers look at the interplay of biological, psychological and social approaches (as a few have), creating a more unified approach to the study of crime. That stated, biological explanations of crime still display a tendency to make grand claims based on little evidence. Biological theories have also fuelled cultural myths such as the perceptions that some racial groups could be considered inferior, and that women could be seen as irrational. Biological theories have also led to the development of eugenics, which proposes removal or containment of those deemed to be inferior (for example, in Nazi Germany non-white races, homosexuals, gypsies, Jews, the mentally ill and the physically disabled were targeted).

> I have suggested that criminological theory was influenced by ideological considerations. Consider the following question: What should we do if we found that it was possible to predict accurately 97% of murderers by finding a 'murder gene'? The answer you would give to this question cannot be fact, but is based upon personal values and beliefs.

Biological criminology has proved very influential, and has not always been associated with the most extreme forms of treatment. It could be argued that the positivistic drive has increased the influence of experts keen to 'treat' and 'rehabilitate' offenders. We refer to this as 'the treatment paradigm' (essentially the idea that criminals should be treated rather than punished).

PSYCHOLOGICAL THEORIES

KEY THINKER

Hans Eysenck (1916–97) Eysenck is best known (in terms of his criminological work) for *Crime and Personality* (1964). Eysenck was a British psychologist (although he was actually born in Berlin during the First World War) who suggested that personality is biologically determined. Having trained under Cyril Burt, Eysenck believed that it was possible to chart the human personality on scales of three core components: extroversion, neuroticism and psychoticism. He believed that exaggeration of these personality traits could lead to greater propensity toward anti-social behaviour.

Another aspect of criminology that locates the cause of crime primarily within the individual is psychology (although some psychology falls into the category of social psychology which acknowledges concepts such as identity, thinking and small group influences that may be external to the individual). 'Psychology' is a term usually used to mean the study of someone's mind or spirit (although sometimes animals are also studied under these headings).

More specifically, psychology is associated with an individual's personality, reasoning, thought, intelligence, learning, perception, imagination, memory and creativity. As with biological theories it is important to remember that psychological theories often make reference to factors that exist outside of the individual. That stated, the core causation of criminality is regarded as existing principally within the individual's 'personality'.

Within the general psychological theories of crime (although it is a theory that is not exclusively concerned with psychology), a most noted thinker was Hans Eysenck. In his work *Crime and Personality* (1964), which is regarded as a work of psychology, Eysenck developed a theory of crime and the causation of crime that linked biological and sociological influences with the development of an individual's personality. Eysenck believed that some people would be more inclined towards anti-social behaviour because of their personality.

Hans Eysenck's *Crime and Personality* (1964)

- Eysenck's theory incorporates biological, social and individual factors.
- He thought that through genetic transmission, some individuals are born with abnormalities of the brain and nervous system that will affect their ability to learn from, or condition themselves to, the environment around them.
- Most children learn to control their behaviour by developing a 'conscience'.
- People have three dimensions of personality: Extroversion (E), Neuroticism
- (N) and Psychoticism (P).
- These dimensions are all charted on a scale (think of a line) that runs between low and high. Most people will fall in the middle range – there will be relatively few people at the extreme ends of the scales.
- Extroverts are under aroused, and therefore someone who is high E will be impulsive and seek stimulation.
- Neuroticism concerns emotions. People who are low N are stable, calm and even tempered (even under stress) while in contrast someone who is a high N would be moody and anxious.
- Psychoticism is difficult to define, but it assesses attributes such as a liking for solitude, aggression and tough mindedness that again range from low to high.
- The speed of people's ability to develop conscience is influenced by their ability to be conditioned, which will depend upon their personality.
- High E and high N individuals are most difficult to condition.
- Low N and Low E are the most receptive to conditioning.
- Those with strong anti-social tendencies will score high on all three scales.

Eysenck's work blended psychological theories with other influences, something that is shared by a great deal of more recent psychological criminology. Indeed it is worth stressing the point that psychology could be linked to any number of other criminological theories. Theories that stress the influence of societal factors, such as economic pressures, peer group influences and self-perception, all rely to some extent upon the way an individual perceives themselves (and therefore must acknowledge the individual's psychology).

More contemporary studies that have attempted to link criminality to individual psychology have attempted to make clear links with other factors, be they sociological, environmental, biological, or a combination of all three. Right-wing American criminologist James Q. Wilson (who is a prominent right realist) produced a general psychological theory of crime in collaboration with Richard J. Herrnstein (a Harvard University professor in psychology). They turned their attention to early social circumstances and family influences in *Crime and Human Nature* (1985).

Wilson and Herrnstein view crime as a rational act of a defective personality. They argue that crime occurs when the rewards (be they material gains, peer approval, emotional gratification, or a sense of justice restored) exceed the costs of imprisonment, pangs of conscience, shame, and so forth. They assert that people differ in how they calculate risks and benefits; to unravel that crucial difference, they analyse a range of factors, including sociological, psychological and environmental.

Ultimately Wilson and Herrnstein reject the biological notion of the existence of a specific gene for criminality. Rather, they postulate that a particular personality type, with features that make a person more likely to value crime, is more likely to be responsible. These features, which the authors call 'constitutional factors', are either inborn or emerge very early in life and are only minimally influenced by family, and even less so by culture and economy. For instance, Wilson and Herrnstein regard impulsiveness and the inability to contemplate the long-term consequences of one's actions as a critical element of the criminal personality. Criminals are stunted in their ability to weight either the costs to be exacted or the future benefits and consequently they opt for the immediate emotional and material gratification.

WHY ARE BIOLOGICAL AND PSYCHOLOGICAL THEORIES INFLUENTIAL?

- Biological positivism, and most psychological criminology, locates the cause of crime predominantly within the individual (and not therefore in economic or social conditions). It is therefore politically useful as it deflects attention away from the demand to improve social and economic conditions.

- Psychiatry as a discipline advanced and gained prestige, providing a suitable backdrop for notions of 'treatment'.
- The concepts are connected with prejudices and fears about 'dangerous classes' amongst more respectable classes, especially in expanding cities in the early twentieth century.
- It offers new possibilities for scientific, humane and expert control and regulation of the population for those in power (governments), when other options seemingly are not working.
- The move towards incarceration as the principal method for dealing with offenders means that there are both subjects for study available (prisoners), and a purpose in studying them to try and inform knowledge and practice.
- Almost all criminological theories can be linked with psychology in some way, whilst biological features are hidden and cannot easily be proved or disproved for the majority of offenders.

CONTEMPORARY PSYCHOLOGICAL THEORIES

While it is possible to regard psychology as passé, the reality is that many contemporary criminal justice practices and interventions are reliant upon psychological principles. For example, most of the forms of contemporary offender treatment and therapy used today in North America and Western Europe derive from psychological work. Similarly, assessment of offender 'risk' is largely based on psychology, and actuarial and structured clinical assessment measures. So too a diverse range of sub-specialisms in criminology are all informed by more nuanced and developed psychological principles largely derived from large-scale and well-resourced quantitative studies. These include: offender profiling (which can assist police investigations); case linkage (also referred to as comparative case analysis and linkage analysis – a process which is regularly conducted by police officers and crime analysts who work for the police, and it is sometimes a task that offender profilers are asked to conduct in order to examine whether separate crimes are likely committed by the same offender); and spatial behaviour profiling (which is used to predict where offenders live, work and socialize, and which is also known as geographical profiling). It is also becoming increasingly common for psychologists to contribute to criminal and civil cases as expert witnesses in court, and to seek to understand topics such as memory recall which are relevant to issues such as the weight which should be given to eye witness testimony. Psychology has also become more attuned to the sociological and environmental factors that are external to the individual but are predictors of criminality. Therefore psychology has become massively influential in criminology, a fact to which an array of recent textbooks attests. The fact that some training in and basic knowledge of psychology has become almost a prerequisite for those working in the statutory agencies of the criminal justice system may be seen to prove its practical usefulness. Psychology still has much to offer criminologists. As Peter Ainsworth has suggested, 'of all the academic disciplines that have examined crime and its causation, psychology seems best placed to help investigators to understand the behaviour of those individuals who commit serious crime' (2001: 184).

'Consider the strength of the argument that criminals are "born not made".'

This type of question would immediately allow you to show knowledge of the development of criminology, and you should remember that you can make reference to Lombroso and his work. However, you should also consider the whole range of factors that can influence criminality (using the upcoming chapters). Remember there is more recent genetic criminology that retains a link with earlier biological criminology and you might want to read further and develop some knowledge of relevant contemporary studies.

Further resources

Excerpts from Lombroso and Eysenck's works are available in McLaughlin et al.'s *Criminological Perspectives* (2003). More generally, a number of textbooks give comprehensive coverage of the subjects of biological and psychological criminology. For example, if you would like to seek to understand more of the influence of psychological approaches you may be interested in Craig Webber's book, *Psychology and Crime* (2009).

2.4   CRIME AS EXTERNAL TO THE INDIVIDUAL: CLASSIC SOCIOLOGICAL THEORIES

Core Areas

Consensus theories

Conflict theories

Feminist perspectives

Social disorganization

Differential association

Strain

Status frustration

Differential opportunity

Neutralization

Drift

Control theory

Labelling/interactionist/new deviancy theories

Realism

Right realism

Left realism

RUNNING THEMES

As most of the theories described below stem from the work of sociologists, they have tended to show a greater awareness of **inequality**, **power**, **class**, **sex and gender**, **race**, **ideology**, **representation**, **discrimination** and **justice** than concern with finding 'causes of crime'. They have also very often (though not always) relied upon different **research methods** to biological and psychological criminology, instead promoting qualitative research with those who offend.

KEY THINKERS

There are quite simply too many influential studies to isolate and examine only a couple of contributions, and therefore I have listed what I consider to be some seminal works. I would draw your attention to the following theorists (although this list is far from exhaustive):

- Durkheim (1952 [1895])
- Sutherland (1937, 1939)
- Tannenbaum (1938)
- Merton (1938, 1968)

- Shaw and McKay (1942)
- Cohen (1955)
- Sykes and Matza (1957)
- Cloward and Ohlin (1960)
- Becker (1963)
- Matza (1964)
- Hirschi (1969)
- Quinney (1970, 1974)
- Lemert (1972)
- Taylor, Walton and Young (1973)
- Wilson (1975)
- Sutherland and Cressey (1978)
- Lea and Young (1984)
- Currie (1985)
- Gottfredson and Hirschi (1990)
- Murray (1990)

The previous section explored attempts by criminologists of both the psychological and biological school to locate the causes of crime specifically within the individual. Such a focus often suggests that there are identifiable differences between offenders and non-offenders. This chapter is devoted to those criminological theorists who have proposed that criminality can perhaps best be understood with reference to social circumstances and factors external to the individual.

CONSENSUS THEORIES

Example: Durkheim (1895)

Several versions of consensus theories thrived in both Europe and America between the late nineteenth century and the 1950s. These theories sought to explain laws against crime as expressions of a consensus of social and moral views. The functionalist view suggests that although crime and deviance are problematic, they can also play an important role in pushing forward moral boundaries. Therefore functionalists can regard crime as a price worth paying for the possibility of progress (this idea is most prominently associated with Emile Durkheim). Consensus and functionalist views take for granted that criminals exist who must be controlled, and do not seek to explain why people behave in the way that they do (although criminal behaviour is not regarded as pathological or abnormal).

CONFLICT THEORIES

Examples: Sellin (1938); Vold (1958); Quinney (1970; 1980 [1977]); and Taylor, Walton and Young (1973)

There have been several versions of conflict theory, which can be regarded as originating in the 1950s, but gained increasing prominence in the 1960s. Like consensus and functionalist approaches, conflict theories are interested in the role that the law serves, and why some things are defined as crime whilst others are not. A number of conflict theorists are mentioned previously, as they contributed a great deal to debates about what crime is. Conflict theories can be divided into groups. Conflict theory in the 1960s became heavily linked with Marxist theory, and tended to emphasize a single dominant source of power that is rooted in control of wealth, but able to influence the ideology of crime and control through the mass media. From the 1960s onward, Marxist criminology and Neo-Marxist theory informed the development of **left idealist** or **radical** criminology. This was an approach informed by sociological theory that sought to take crime seriously, but still analyse why some people and some actions were deemed criminal, and the role of the state and the powerful in this process. Left idealists believed that research should be critical, and seek to highlight the divisions in society. That stated, Marxism has become an unfashionable theoretical basis, and few criminologists would now suggest that they were left idealist in their theoretical perspective. In the 1990s, conflict theories focused more upon issues of racial discrimination and institutional racism in the processing of Black and Asian offenders. In Britain the best example is still Taylor, Walton and Young's *The New Criminology* (1973) and in America, Richard Quinney's 1970 and 1974 studies.

FEMINIST PERSPECTIVES

Examples: Adler (1975) and Smart (1976)

There is not a single feminist theory of crime. Feminism draws from other theories (especially conflict theory) to describe the way females are affected by the criminal justice system (women's experiences both as offenders and victims). The reason that we refer to feminist perspectives (and not feminist theory) is that there are many different versions of feminism. Feminists also often make use of the concept of 'patriarchy', to describe the structural oppression of women that exists within society.

Although there are a range of feminist perspectives, almost all feminist perspectives share a concern with the inequality of women, discrimination against them and an insistence that, all too often, theories neglect women, and assume that theories about male behaviour are applicable to the experiences of women.

From the 1970s on, feminist criminologists argued that criminology either neglected women, or explained women's behaviour in stereotypical and discriminatory ways. For example, they highlighted the fact that biological explanations that had long been discredited as explanations for male criminal behaviour were still being applied to women. Feminists also raised questions about whether women were unfairly treated by the criminal justice system, for example, by getting longer sentences for less serious offences. That stated, the extent to which the criminal justice system discriminates against women is contested, and feminist theorists are still very influential in criminology.

Similarly, gender debates have not been restricted to why women commit crime, but have also questioned why men disproportionately commit more crime, and whether this may be because of crime's potential for reinforcing a masculine image. Many of these debates are not put forward by female feminists but by males who endorse feminist philosophy and take a pro-feminist stance (both these aspects are examined in more detail in Chapter 2.9).

SOCIAL DISORGANIZATION

Example: Shaw and McKay (1942)

Those who subscribe to social disorganization theory suggest that stability and integration into society produce conformity in people. Conversely, disorder and poor integration can permit and encourage crime.

The Chicago School of Sociology

Social disorganization theory is linked with the University of Chicago's School of Sociology (often referred to as the Chicago School) and originated in the 1920s. A number of influential sociologists/criminologists from the Chicago School used social disorganization theory in their work (there are a number of examples in other chapters: Shaw and McKay (1942), Thrasher (1927) and Sutherland (1939), to name but some). The influence of the Chicago School could be seen as being both methodological and theoretical. The University of Chicago's contribution to criminology often begins by acknowledging the work of Robert E. Park and Ernest W. Burgess. Park was an influential figure who encouraged students to undertake qualitative research in the field. Burgess is perhaps more notable as a theoretical criminologist than Park, having taught the first criminology and delinquency courses at the University of Chicago. Park and Burgess (with McKenzie) authored *The City* in 1925 – this book introduced the theory of 'concentric circles' upon which the criminological theory of social disorganization is built.

I have known a number of criminology courses set assignments where students are asked to evaluate the contribution of the Chicago School to criminology. The role of the Chicago School was not simply social disorganization and a lasting focus upon the link between the environment and crime. Chicago theorists were instrumental in promoting qualitative research methods, e.g. Thrasher and participant observation (1927); Shaw and life history (1930). The Chicago School's contribution to criminology in terms of research methods should not be overlooked!

Social disorganization is most readily associated with ecological studies of delinquency undertaken by Clifford R. Shaw and Henry D. McKay (1942), which in turn owe much to the rapid expansion of Chicago as a city, and link patterns of juvenile delinquency to patterns of urban development and the expansion of the city. Delinquency and deviance were regarded as higher in areas near the city centre. At the heart of the city was industry and business, but as the city grew, these businesses encroached into what were once residential areas. The area that surrounds the city, the 'zone of transition', was often associated with migrant groups that were the most recent arrivals to the city. This area was characterized by the poorest (often rented) housing, physical decay, broken communities, a shifting and transient population and high rates of illegitimate birth. Those from the Chicago School suggested that crime was not the result of biological and psychological abnormalities. Instead, Chicago theorists believed that crime and deviance were normal responses to these abnormal environmental circumstances. They suggested that crime could be 'culturally transmitted' across generations, and that industrialization, urbanization and to some extent migration (and the resulting lack of attachment to community and institutions) undermine stability.

The policy implications of accepting social disorganization essentially involve working in communities (particularly in high delinquency areas), increasing informal social control, encouraging young people to form an attachment to their community, and challenging delinquent energies into legitimate leisure pursuits. Whilst social disorganization is not empirically proven, much would seem to support what people think. Researchers are still influenced by the link between urban development and environment and crime, with modern crime prevention researchers paying a great deal of attention to environment and crime.

DIFFERENTIAL ASSOCIATION

Examples: Sutherland (1939); Sutherland and Cressey (1978)

Edwin Sutherland, a Chicago School sociologist, made many contributions to criminology, one of which is the concept of differential association. It was Sutherland (1939), and in collaboration with Cressey (1978), who suggested that criminal behaviour was learnt and transmitted. He was influenced by a desire that criminology should examine crime as socially harmful, and include the crime of the socially elite (see Chapter 2.11).

Differential association theory asserts that criminal behaviour is learned rather than inherited or invented by individuals. It is learned in social interaction, often within intimate social groups. Differential association suggests that a person becomes delinquent because of exposure to attitudes and ideas favourable to violations of law (as opposed to unfavourable) in their surrounding subculture. Differential association also suggests that the process of learning by association with criminal and anti-criminal patterns does not involve imitation alone. The longer or more frequently an individual is exposed to attitudes and behaviour, the more affect that attitude or behaviour is likely to have upon the individual. Sutherland did not suggest that the goals or desires of offenders were different to those of society more generally, simply that they had different ways of achieving their aims.

Differential association stresses the interactions between individuals and the influence of significant others upon them, but also stresses the importance of learning. It has, therefore, a physiological component and is often regarded as psychological criminology. It is consequently one example of the difficulty in separating theories into categories under broad headings.

STRAIN

Example: Merton (1938; 1968)

Anomie is a concept that stems from the work of functionalist Emile Durkheim, and means a state of confusion about social rules and values that is often caused by rapid social change. Durkheim first developed the concept as part of his attempt to explain suicide, but in terms of criminology it is perhaps more relevant to turn to the work of the American sociologist Robert Merton, set out to explain the reasons for crime being concentrated in lower-class areas, and in lower-class and minority groups. He also sought to explain why the USA had such a high crime rate.

Merton argued that there was an inequality between culturally-approved goals in society (an example of a goal is that all men are encouraged to pursue success in terms of wealth and status) and the means of achieving those goals (the means of achieving wealth and status through, say, education and employment, are not open to everyone). Merton argued that this disparity (or strain) between means and goals drove some of those denied the legal or legitimate means, to turn to illegal means. Therefore strain creates frustration and resentment, and this is the motive for crime.

Robert Agnew is one of the theorists inspired by Merton's concept of strain, and he attempted to focus more directly upon the impact of 'strain' upon individuals (1992). Agnew reworked Merton's notion of strain into three types, and produced a version of strain theory that paid more attention to the psychological impacts of strain.

In terms of policy, the existence of strain can lead to a promotion of social justice, trying to provide for an equality of opportunity for all, and promotion of less competitiveness.

STATUS FRUSTRATION

Examples: Cohen (1955); Agnew (1992); Messerschmidt (1993)

Linking with strain and the concept of anomie is the notion of status frustration. This concept is in essence descended from strain and deals with the way illegitimate rather than legitimate activities are endorsed by some groups (which often includes the lower class, the disadvantaged and excluded minorities who feel the wrongness of being denied the legitimate opportunities that others have). Status frustration is informed by a need to aspire to a form of behaviour that weakens any commitment to lead a law-abiding life.

Evidence which supports this notion is often qualitative and ethnographic, conforming to what is referred to as gang and subculture studies. For example, Albert Cohen (1955) was particularly interested in the crimes of delinquent males who often offended together. Particularly, Cohen provides some explanation as to why there exists a 'delinquent subculture' amongst lower-class males. His work was conducted in America in the 1950s. Cohen suggested that lower-class males in that society often could not aspire, legally, to the material standards of the middle class in terms of dress, behaviour, educational success and gainful employment. Cohen argued that this denied them status in society and could serve to lower their self-esteem. He argued that in particular, lower-class males came into contact with middle-class values in school. Here they had a choice. They could conform (and possibly become losers), or they could reject the standards of the middle class, and celebrate and enact the opposite values. Cohen argued that young lower-class males could invert the values of middle-class society and thereby create their own system of standards, which in turn created self-esteem. The motives for delinquent behaviour are anger and resentment. In creating their own subculture, young lower-class males place value upon meeting the expectation of peers rather than teachers and parents. Subcultures become self-reinforcing, a permanent alternative to middle-class standards. Therefore 'status frustration' contributes to delinquency, with youngsters offending out of 'malice' and 'for the hell of it'. Status frustration can also cross with subjects such as masculinity and crime, and James Messerschmidt's concept of young men offending to 'do masculinity' (1993) also fits this model.

DIFFERENTIAL OPPORTUNITY

Example: Cloward and Ohlin (1960)

In the 1960s in America, Richard Cloward and Lloyd Ohlin contributed their perspective to the debate about lower-class youth subcultures with the theory of 'differential opportunity'. Their theory attempted to bridge the Merton **strain theory** and Sutherland **differential association** (interestingly, Ohlin had formerly studied under Sutherland, whilst Cloward had been taught by Merton).

Cloward and Ohlin believed that Cohen may have been right about subcultures possessing different values to those of the middle class, but there was more than one type of subculture. Similarly, while influenced by Merton,

Cloward and Ohlin questioned whether everyone denied opportunity to legitimate success could in fact turn to illegitimate means. They believed that there were variations in the availability of illegitimate means to people. While Sutherland had argued that criminality was caused by differential association, Cloward and Ohlin suggested that delinquent subcultures were based upon different opportunities that existed in different neighbourhoods. They suggested three separate subcultures (two of which were for society's excluded losers, see below).

Differential opportunity suggests three separate subcultures

Criminal	Conflict	Retreatist
(Making a living)	(Gang fighting)	(Drugs and alcohol)

All of the theories derived from anomie tend to predict higher rates of delinquency in lower-class and excluded groups. Whilst official statistics would seem to support this assertion, official statistics are notoriously unreliable (see Chapter 2.6). There are a number of reasons why crime might be seen as more common in lower-class males – most notably that it is young lower-class males who live in the areas in which the police tend to go looking for crime. It is also true that those from lower-class and disadvantaged backgrounds tend to be treated more harshly than their middle-class counterparts (e.g. they are more likely to be prosecuted, and more likely to receive more serious sanctions).

Self-report studies (mass surveys that are undertaken in confidence) show some minor youthful offending is distributed quite evenly across social class (although serious and persistent crime that tends to continue into adulthood is more common amongst the disadvantaged). There are problems with self-report studies, but the contradiction that this presents is an interesting one. There are also problems with the terms that are used. Disadvantaged and excluded are often linked to unemployment, however there is little evidence that suggests that unemployment alone leads to crime.

Anomie might also tend to exaggerate the extent to which people are passive actors influenced by society's goals. Many ordinary people may not take seriously the glamorous goals of society and instead measure themselves against more realistic and achievable goals – therefore not feeling aggrieved or frustrated. In terms of class and the definitions of class, perhaps the definitions of 'middle' and 'working class' are too general, how we define class is debatable, and there may be overlaps between class groups and values. Similarly, anomie theories tend to be predominantly urban in terms of their scope, and do not really tend to sit comfortably with urbanized, westernized society. In terms of scope it is questionable as to whether anomie theories seek to explain general patterns of criminal activity or the 'criminal careers' of individuals. Similarly, the criminologists that produced anomie linked to delinquent subcultures studied only men and boys, no one explained the differential distribution of crime between men and women – gender and its role in crime was not sufficiently explored. All of these factors serve to make the theories uncertain, even if to a large extent they may seem plausible and persuasive.

NEUTRALIZATION

Example: Sykes and Matza (1957)

Gresham Sykes and David Matza introduced their theory of neutralization at the time when studies of subculture were most dominant, and theories based upon anomie were prevalent. Cohen and Cloward and Ohlin suggested that delinquents and criminals were able to act in such a way because they rejected society's 'norms' and 'values' and replaced them with their own value system. In other words, by obeying their own 'codes', which were different to those of mainstream society, criminals could feel no guilt. Sykes and Matza did not believe that this was the case. They did not believe that delinquents wholly rejected society's values, replacing them with their own; rather they simply found a way to get around them. The way they did this was by employing a series of attitudes that served to rationalize and justify their behaviour. These were 'techniques of neutralization'.

DRIFT

Example: Matza (1964)

Matza built upon the 'techniques of neutralization' with a more general theory that attempted to explain juvenile involvement in crime. He maintained the stance that total rejection of society's norms was not necessary for a delinquent to commit a criminal act. Highlighting the concept of free will, Matza suggested that people could choose criminal and non-criminal actions. Matza argued that adolescents drift between conventional and criminal behaviour, not necessarily occupying one position, but instead choosing when to be criminal and when not to be. The techniques of neutralization simply freed the individual from conventional society values and helped them to commit crime.

CONTROL THEORY

Examples: Hirschi (1969); Gottfredson and Hirschi (1990)

Control theory approaches the issue of crime from a slightly different angle than many other criminological theories. It does not ask why people become criminals, but asks why people obey the law. The answer is to be found in control. People conform because they are controlled, and offend when this control breaks down. Control theory therefore tends to take crime for granted, as a given – people do not need a special motivation to commit a crime. Rather, much like classicism, control theory suggests that anyone can offend, but sees individuals as even more self-interested and self-absorbed – 'anyone will violate the law if they think that they can get away with it'.

Control theory is most often associated with Travis Hirschi's *Causes of Delinquency* (1969) which used data gathered from a study of adolescent delinquents in California, and proposes that 'delinquent acts result when an individual's bond to society is weak or broken' (1969: 16). Control theory can be used to explain any type of criminal behaviour or delinquency. It has been utilized and has influenced all manner of criminological discussion, and perhaps occupies the position of the most frequently discussed and tested of all criminological theories.

The core concept of control theory is the individual's bond to society. The bond has four component parts:

1   **Attachment** – including admiring and identifying with others so that we care about the expectations they have. The more insensitive an individual is to other people's expectations, the more they disregard their norms and the more likely they are to violate them. The concept of attachment is often linked to parenting.
2   **Commitment** – the extent to which individuals have invested in conventional norms and have a stake in conformity, which might be jeopardized by crime. Essentially, the more someone has to lose, the less likely they are to risk criminality.

3   **Involvement** – relating to the idea that the more preoccupied an individual is with accepted and conventional activities, the less likely they are to have the time, energy and contacts to get involved in unconventional activities. It follows that working, spending time with the family and participation in structured leisure activities all serve to reduce the likelihood to engage in criminality.

4   **Agreement** – if a person finds the laws agreeable, they are less likely to break them. If a person endorses society's rules, they will not go against them (this component is termed 'conformity').

In his work, Hirschi supplied measurable criteria that could be used to evaluate individuals against all of the bonds. He tested his own theory and argued that the weaker the bonds, the higher the delinquency. Since the late 1960s, research has generally supported (to varying degrees) Hirschi's general propositions. That stated, whilst control theory might explain a significant proportion of delinquency, some people who are strongly attached offend, whilst some of those who are not, do not. Hirschi himself later rejected his own theory, and working jointly with Gottfredson (1990) moved toward a more simple theory of self-control, arguing that people with low self-control commit more crime (low self-control involved poor socialization, especially poor child-rearing, poor quality of or lack of parental discipline, and was closely linked to the family).

LABELLING/INTERACTIONIST/NEW DEVIANCY THEORIES

Examples: Tannenbaum (1938); Becker (1963); Lemert (1972)

According to the interactionist school, crime and deviance can be explained as the result of a social reaction process that individuals go through in order to become deviant. It is rooted in symbolic interactionism, a sociological concept that suggests that individuals acquire their sense of 'self' through interacting with others.

Interactionist criminology is associated with Tannenbaum, Lemert and Becker. These theorists essentially argued that the labels given to deviants or offenders by those with power are a factor that can serve to reinforce, and create criminality. Individuals can be dramatically stigmatized by the use of labels. The labels attached by the criminal justice system through court processes and sanctions, and the labels of the mental health system, are amongst the most powerful, and the label can serve to amplify deviance.

Perhaps the term 'labelling' does not instantly appear in contemporary debates such as the stereotyping of black and female offenders, sex offenders and paedophiles, but it is possible to regard labelling as a precursor to these current concerns. Labelling is a very useful concept when any group is talked about in stereotypical terms.

REALISM

Realist criminology tends to be either politically right or left in its ideology, but regardless of political affiliation, both sides of realist criminology share some common beliefs about crime and its 'reality'. Essentially, as crime rates rose in Britain and North America from the 1960s onwards there was a concern that conflict theories and sociological explanations failed to address the causes.

Remember that realist criminology, whatever its political affiliation, is characterized by a belief that:

- crime had risen from the 1960s in both America and Britain
- crime is a problem which has a destructive and negative impact upon communities
- there is the need for academic criminologists to produce research that helps to develop realistic policy that will feed into practices that counter the 'crime problem'.

Further resources

It is difficult to understand the emergence of realism if you do not understand the way that law and order entered into political debate in Britain and America, but there are few texts that chart the politicization of law and order. One exception is David Downes and Rod Morgan's chapter 'Dumping the "hostages to fortune"?' This appears in the second edition of the *Oxford Handbook of Criminology* (Maguire et al., 1997). It is well worth trying to access this through your university library as it provides an excellent overview of the politicization of law and order.

RIGHT REALISM

Examples: Wilson (1975); Wilson and Herrnstein (1985); Murray (1990)

Right realism (sometimes known as neo-conservative or neo-classical criminology) is associated principally with American academics such as James Q. Wilson and Charles Murray. Prominent right realists tend to have academic backgrounds in politics and political theory. This fostered a belief that there was a necessity for criminological theory to generate ideas that were useful to policy-makers.

Wilson believed that crime was a choice that followed the simple principles of economics – 'if crime pays more people will do it, if it pays less, less people will do it' (1975: 117). The way to achieve a reduction in crime therefore was to make crime pay less by the swift removal of society's persistent criminals for a significant proportion of their criminal career. Such action, argued Wilson, should lead to a changed perception amongst those likely to offend, and therefore crime would be less frequent.

Wilson's commonsense approach owed much to literary flair, and it has often been argued that his writing (and that of other right realists) is highly opinion based, with less emphasis placed upon evidence. Perhaps a counter to this is the fact that because many right realist thinkers come from 'philosophical' backgrounds there is less emphasis placed upon undertaking research, and so they are keen to generate arguments based upon moral reasoning and economics.

Another prominent right realist, Charles Murray, argued that in the lowest status groups in society, welfare dependency and 'fecklessness' had created a two tier system of poor. One group of poor were willing to advance themselves and adhere to society's values; the other type ('the underclass') were not. Murray located the causation of the rising crime problem in America and Britain within this 'underclass'. The solution, for Murray, involved the retreat of state government, giving self-government opportunities to poor and affluent communities alike, and greater responsibility for the operation of institutions that affect their lives (1990). Whilst Murray's thesis on the underclass is doubtless of importance, he is also noted for advocating the effectiveness of imprisonment on the grounds of deterrence, and coined the phrase 'prison works' shortly before it was used by Michael Howard in his now famous speech at the Conservative Party Conference in 1993.

The key points of right realism

- Crime is freely chosen (hence right realism is sometimes called right classicism).
- Minor crime leads to more substantial crimes, but hardline approaches that deter and prevent societal decline can also prevent crime.
- Academic theory should be used to inform policy-making.
- Crimes of the 'street' concern the public most and must be targeted.
- The 'underclass' (welfare dependant, criminal and illegitimate) are those most responsible for rises in crime rates in Britain and America (Murray, 1990), however bothersome and unruly people (such as drunks, beggars and the mentally ill) also contribute (Wilson and Kelling, 1982).
- The state should withdraw from delivery of service and promote self-government with people having a greater say in services, but principles based upon deterrence are most effective in terms of criminal justice interventions.
- Prison and 'zero tolerance' strategies are effective at reducing crime rates.

LEFT REALISM

Examples: Lea and Young (1984); Currie (1985)

Left realism essentially stems from left idealist and conflict criminology, and began with criminologists in Britain, who in the 1980s proposed a shift toward a more 'realistic' stance on crime.

Left realists rejected what they saw as punitive and exclusionary policies that were endorsed by right realists and sought to counter to the growing influence of the mainly American right realists. They also rejected many of the policies of the right-wing governments of Thatcher and Reagan, but argued that 'conflict criminology' based upon Marxism, and labelling theories were unrealistic in their appraisal of crime (they believed such criminology displayed a tendency to shift attention from the actions of offenders, regarding them as victims). They promoted a politically left-leaning view of crime, with a number of the left realists formerly having subscribed to left idealist principles (most notably Jock Young).

Like right realists, left realists agreed that crimes of the 'street' caused the public alarm and concern, and consequently they attempted to move away from some of the more radical political ideas associated with 'conflict' criminology.

Left realism differs from right realism in that it does not accept that choice and free will are the sole factors in terms of causation of crime. They suggest that in order to study and understand crime, it needs to be broken down into four component parts (these form the square of crime, which is shown below). The square of crime represents the interconnected elements that constitute crime and therefore any analysis of crime must make reference to these components. Crime constitutes a social relationship between each of the four corners of the square. So, for example, the relationship between the state and the public determines the effectiveness of policing; the relationship between victim and offender will have an effect upon the impact of the crime; the relationship between offender and state will effect whether further crimes are committed; and the relationship between these four points will vary, dependent upon the crime.

Table 2.3

The square of crime	State (Control agencies)	Offender
	Social Control	**Criminal Act**
	The Public	Victim/s

A further key concept for the left realists was that of relative deprivation, which suggests that it is not the level or degree of poverty that caused crime, but it is the sense of injustice and disadvantage, which exclusion creates, that is instrumental in creating the conditions in which crime occurs. Left realism has been important in promoting the notion of 'social exclusion' which has been an ongoing concern of the government since 1997.

The key points of left realism

- Left realism attempts to find a middle ground between right realism and left idealism, criticising the exclusionary and punitive nature of the right, along with the unrealistic idealism of conflict and left idealist criminology.

- Left realism has an evidence base which involves the use of victimization surveys that suggest that the poorest and most excluded are those who most suffered the effects of crime. It regards 'relative deprivation' as a cause of crime, rather than poverty generally.
- Left realism is an inclusive philosophy that acknowledges the contribution of subcultural theory, labelling theory, feminist and conflict theories.
- Left realism suggests that the best responses to crime involve a variety of actors in social crime prevention, i.e. 'multi-agency' responses (although left realism also acknowledges that situational crime prevention and deterrent principles can be effective). Its long-term goal is to make long-term changes in the way society operates in terms of equality and justice, but similarly to 'protect the public' on a day-to-day basis.

All of the theories discussed above have a sociological component, that is, all recognize that crime is not simply a product of free will, and that other factors that exist in society can impact upon an individual's propensity toward crime.

'How have sociological theories contributed to criminology?'

One of the problems that I tend to encounter with this type of question is that students will tend to try too hard and do too much in very little detail, rather than examine one or two theories in much greater detail. I would suggest that the latter approach is often better, as it allows you to convey an appreciation of one theory in detail. For example, you could take strain theory, talk about Merton, and then how Agnew built upon his work. You could make reference to the types of crime where strain may be evident. It is always far better, I feel, to be specific and show a good level of understanding of one theme.

Further resources

There are a wide range of sources mentioned in this chapter, which reflects the eclectic nature of criminology. I am firmly of the belief that students of criminology can benefit most from reading some of the original works mentioned above. That stated, I recognize that this is a time-consuming

(Continued)

(Continued)

endeavour and therefore would recommend McLaughlin et al.'s *Criminological Perspectives* (2003) where you will encounter a number of extracts from works mentioned above.

David Downes and Paul Rock's *Understanding Deviance* (2011) is now in its sixth edition and is an excellent comprehensive textbook, and Katherine Williams also gives an excellent coverage in her textbook, *Criminology* (2004). Those wishing to access a more interesting account of sociological contributions to criminology might consider Smith and Natalier's *Understanding Criminal Justice: Sociological Perspectives* (2004) as this contains some interesting contributions that are not acknowledged by many criminological textbooks.

2.5   CONTEMPORARY CRIMINOLOGY

CORE AREAS

Administrative criminology

Routine activity theory

Experimental criminology

Peacemaking criminology

Cultural criminology

Green and environmental criminology

Convict criminology

Postmodern and late-modern criminology

Comparative criminology

Psychosocial criminology

Crime science

RUNNING THEMES

This chapter charts the development of some of the criminological theories that have emerged in recent years; and therefore I have termed it contemporary criminology. However, this should not be taken to signify that the theories in this chapter are any more or less relevant than those that you have encountered so far. Rather they are the more recent theories that have emerged in what is a constantly evolving academic subject. Due to the wide range of theories incorporated under this heading you should keep in mind the running themes generally and consider them in the context of each theory.

KEY THINKERS

This list is not meant as an exhaustive list of key thinkers (there are a great many names that could appear on this list!). Instead it seeks to direct you to some relevant contemporary examples:

- Pepinsky and Quinney (1991)
- Cornish and Clarke (1996)
- Clarke (1997)
- Felson and Clarke (1998)
- Ferrell, Hayward and Young (2008)
- Sherman (2009)

ADMINISTRATIVE CRIMINOLOGY

Examples: Cornish and Clarke (1996); Clarke (1997)

Administrative criminology gained influence in Britain from the late 1970s onward and is linked with realist approaches that sought practical solutions to the 'problem' of crime. Administrative criminology is so termed because of its links with governmental administration. Administrative criminology tends to have little interest in the causes of crime, endorsing the view of Wilson that crime is a rational and calculated choice made by offenders. The solution to crime for administrative criminologists such as Ron Clarke and Marcus Felson was to increase the chances of offenders being caught and to put in place measures that would be likely to increase the risks of being caught in the act of offending, or physically prevent offending (we term such approaches situational crime prevention).

Further resources

Like right and left realism, administrative criminology focuses exclusively upon street and property offences (street theft and robbery, car theft, assault and burglaries). It promotes community and individual responsibility for crime prevention, along with the perceived need to rethink the state's responses to crime, in order to make them more economically viable, more efficient and more effective. Administrative criminology is therefore aligned with research that attempts to ask 'what works?' in the context of offender treatment.

The key points of administrative criminology

- Administrative criminology is a term that is used to describe criminology that refers to the act of committing the crime, and regards the criminal as a rational actor who will make choices.
- It seeks not to solve a problem of crime, but to find ways of preventing crime – or making crime a less attractive prospect for offenders through physical or psychological measures.
- Administrative criminology is so termed due to its close ties with government; it tends to be positivistic in nature, and concerned with situational crime prevention and the efficiency and effectiveness of interventions.

ROUTINE ACTIVITY THEORY

Example: Felson (2002)

Routine activity theory is a sub-field of rational choice criminology, developed by Marcus Felson and often associated and strongly linked with rational choice and administrative criminology.

The premise of routine activity theory (RAT) is that crime is relatively unaffected by social causes such as poverty, inequality, or unemployment. For instance, after the Second World War, the economy of the United States and the United Kingdom expanded alongside state welfare. During that time, crime rose significantly. According to criminologists such as Felson this was because the prosperity of contemporary society offers so much opportunity for crime: there is much more to steal. Routine activity theory is controversial among criminologists who believe in the social causes of crime. This is in part because routine activity theorists such as Marcus Felson are critical of criminologists who suggest that crime is socially constructed. He is a fierce advocate of criminology having to offer practical solutions. Routine activity theory suggests that for crime to be committed, three aspects are needed: 1) a motivated offender; 2) a suitable target; 3) the lack of a capable guardian. The last element, the lack of a capable guardian, need not necessarily be a person (nor does the suitable target), but can refer to a range of factors that routine activity theorists consider would deter a motivated offender from offending in that circumstance. Similarly, the target relates to examples of objects and environmental designs that also act as a guardians or security measures to deter motivated offenders. Therefore RAT branches into the realm of Crime Prevention through Environmental Design (CPTED) where seemingly small measures like the addition of lights, locks, and security cameras act as the capable guardian and can prevent crime against a suitable target. It is also now often part of the evaluation of 'experimental criminology'.

Key points of rational choice criminology

- Crime is the result of the coming together of a motivated offender, a suitable target and the lack of a capable guardian.
- Crime Prevention through Environmental Design (CPTED) can provide the role of capable guardian and reduce crime rates.
- Crime is largely not the product of social factors.
- Technological advances and shifts are core to understanding fluctuating and changing patterns of crime and criminal practices.

EXPERIMENTAL CRIMINOLOGY

Example: Sherman (2009)

Experimental criminology promotes the use of scientific methods, and particularly the use of the randomized controlled trial. The RCT is a specific type of scientific experiment, often used to test the efficacy of various types of intervention within a population (they are often used in health settings). The key distinguishing feature of the usual RCT is that study subjects, after assessment of eligibility and recruitment, but before the intervention to be studied begins, are randomly allocated to receive one or other of the alternative interventions under study. After randomization, the two (or more) groups of subjects are followed in exactly the same way, and the only differences between the interventions they receive, for example, in terms of procedures, should be those intrinsic to the treatments being compared. For example, in criminology it might involve increasing police attendance at some areas and not others, to see if crime can be said to fall with police presence. Experimental criminological research is also notable in that, unlike much traditional criminology, it has the stated aim of assisting in the development of evidence-based crime and justice policy. For example, leading experimental criminologist Lawrence Sherman has suggested that the discipline can create an 'emotionally intelligent' approach to criminal justice, and that 'governments can refuse to waste money on ineffective sanctions despite populist pressures [and] a world in which citizens can demand that government must test policies with well-controlled experiments before spending vast sums in the name of crime prevention' (Sherman, 2009: 7). However, some critics have suggested that rather than being liberating, experimental criminology can become tied to the workings of repressive state practices and fail to recognize that increased liberty is not the inevitable outcome of experimental criminology, especially if the practices it evaluates are effective but intrusive and liberty curtailing. In addition, others question the applicability of such scientific methodology to the realities of crime, much as with traditional forms of administrative criminology.

Key points of experimental criminology

- Largely embraces administrative and rational choice theories.
- Randomized controlled experiments can tell us much about the effectiveness of criminal justice interventions.
- Criminology should embrace the aim of assisting in the development of evidence-based crime and justice policy.
- Governments should test criminal justice policies and practices with well-controlled RCT experiments.

PEACEMAKING CRIMINOLOGY

Example: Pepinsky and Quinney (1991)

The specific concept of 'peacemaking' in criminology was introduced in the US by Harold Pepinsky and Richard Quinney in their book *Criminology as*

Peacemaking (1991) but has had little, if any, impact upon British criminology. They suggested that peacemaking criminology is drawn from three peacemaking traditions: religious, humanistic and feminist/critical.

The core concept of peacemaking criminology is the rejection of what is perceived to be an inherently violent and hierarchical criminal justice system that seeks to redress harm through harm and repress criminality through force. Peacemaking criminologists propose that an alternative, non-oppressive, and inclusive system would be more socially just and acceptable. I would assert that rather than thinking of peacemaking criminology as a new discipline, it is regarded as a long established tradition.

Peacemaking criminologists often reject the language and imagery that accompanies practices in criminal justice, such as the idea of a 'War on Drugs' or 'War on Crime' (which is often linked to right realist criminology), in favour of more considered 'ways of thinking, speaking, and writing that foster peace'; their aim is to build 'a compassionate criminology' (Quinney, 1993: 4). Its ideology could also be regarded as being very much in line with restorative justice philosophies, and a number of current interventions could be regarded as conforming to the general ideas of peacemaking criminology (for example, restorative justice schemes, circles of support and accountability for sex offenders and therapeutic community regimes in prisons).

The key points of peacemaking criminology

- Peacemaking criminology seeks to challenge the inherent violence involved in the criminal and criminal justice process.
- Peacemaking criminologists reject the hierarchical, violent and harmful nature of much criminology, and attempt to isolate, identify and subdue offenders through oppressive practices.
- Peacemaking criminologists reject the notion of solving harms by inflicting harms, and seek a more socially just criminal justice system, particularly promoting inclusion, by attempting to bring people together collectively.
- Peacemaking criminology has been criticized, however. It is perhaps not so much a criminological theory as an attitude or viewpoint. Others have suggested as an ideology it is one associated with privilege and lack of understanding of the realities of the world. Similarly, many criminologists would not consider themselves as 'peacemaking', and it is perhaps a term that is more appropriate for some specific works by criminologists rather than a term used to describe the authors more generally.

CULTURAL CRIMINOLOGY

Examples: Ferrell, Hayward and Young (2008)

Cultural criminology is often regarded as *the* emerging theoretical concept. Its origins can be contested, and are drawn from a range of theoretical traditions such as those of the Chicago School and 'interactionist criminology' and the work of the Birmingham Centre for Contemporary Cultural Studies in the 1970s. Cultural criminology in its most extreme form promotes the formulation of a criminological *Verstehen* where the researcher attempts to understand (perhaps even sympathetically) the emotions and meanings that are associated with crime and crime control.

Cultural criminologists are keen to stress the lived realities of crime, with its adrenaline, its pleasure, its visual impact and feeling, and often set themselves in direct opposition to more scientific and rational choice colleagues. Cultural criminology takes its lead from the growth in cultural studies as a separate area of academic inquiry, and advances and changes in media culture. The subject matter for cultural studies draws upon a range of theoretical concepts that ranges from feminism to film studies, although increasingly it is associated with new techniques of ethnography. Ferrell and Saunders captured the early essence of the ethos of 'cultural criminology', stressing the link between popular culture, style and criminality. They argued that 'the collective practice of criminality and the criminalization of everyday life...are cultural enterprises' (1995: 7).

Cultural criminology is a fairly new addition to criminological theory, but is growing increasingly popular. It analyses issues of representation, meaning and politics in relation to crime and criminal justice, focusing specifically on how the current epoch must be understood via engagement with everyday transgression, popular culture, and the ways in which processes linked to and stemming from consumerism and globalization have created new forms of crime and transgression which require new understanding (Ferrell et al., 2008). It is therefore in keeping with the more sociological traditions of studying crime, deviance and the social control of behaviour, but updated for a new and rapidly changing world. However, for some critics – particularly those associated with more 'scientific' branches of contemporary criminology – it is seen as nothing new, and some have suggested that it is simply a return to old celebratory accounts of deviance.

The key points of cultural criminology

- At its most basic level, 'cultural criminology' draws its influence from 'cultural studies' and imports the insights of cultural studies into criminology.
- Cultural criminology is associated with subcultural studies and ethnography, along with research methods drawn from cultural studies such as media and cultural analysis, or a combination of these methods.
- Cultural criminologists regard crime as a shared and collective experience involving symbols and meanings, collective ideas and identity, human communication and interaction, emotion and feelings.
- Much cultural criminology is in almost direct opposition to administrative, positivistic and realist criminology.

GREEN AND ENVIRONMENTAL CRIMINOLOGY

Example: Beirne and South (2007)

Green and environmental criminology suggests that we reappraise more traditional notions of crimes and start to consider the social harms that societies (including corporations and governments) play in creating or promoting environmental degradation and damage. Criminology is starting to recognize the finite nature of the earth's resources, and with increased concern about global warming, environmental damage and pollution as a context, criminologists have returned to a wider zemiologist concern with such harms as crime, and how new problems of damage and harm can be incorporated into criminological inquiry, with 'green crimes'– in which the environment becomes degraded through human behaviour – as the primary focus and new legislative targeting in recent years. These new categories of green crimes include, for example, crimes of air pollution, deforestation, species decline and against animal rights, and crimes of water pollution. Beyond this, green criminologists are also concerned with state-sponsored acts of violence, intimidation and social control as directed against environmental activists or groups.

Green criminologists argue that criminology similarly needs to be reminded of this absence of social thinking about the environment, and suggest that it is vital to add a green perspective to criminology as it offers another possibility for enrichment of the field, as well as reflecting an awareness about vital twenty-first-century issues, as globalized capitalism accelerates. They have therefore promoted understandings of how air pollution may be a more pressing issue (and more harmful globally) than traditional street crimes, and attempted to shift criminological focus onto issues such as the potential harms of genetically modified food. Green criminology is not simply about promoting green ideas, however. Indeed, a criticism made of traditional green thinking by some criminologists is that it was essentially corporate compliant and simply bought a manipulated, consumerist form of green ideology that often stemmed from offending corporations, and which suggested that people could be green simply by purchasing the correct products, a form of consumerist brainwashing some term 'greenwashing'. Hence green criminology perhaps owes much heredity not only to environmental activism but to the classic traditions of critical criminology that some academic commentators were keen to see dismissed in favour of 'realism' and the politics of right and left.

Indeed, looking ahead to the next century it is unarguable that crime and issues of the environment will be increasingly interwoven; be it through the policing of anti-airport protests, to efforts to curb trade in endangered species or the illegal dumping of toxic waste, a whole new future for green criminological research is on the horizon.

Key points of green criminology

- New crimes of air pollution, deforestation, species decline and against animal rights, and crimes of water pollution.
- Green criminologists argue that criminology needs to be reminded of the absence of social thinking about the environment, and suggest that it is vital to add a green perspective to criminology.
- Societies (including corporations and governments) play a part in creating or promoting environmental degradation and damage, but this is often not considered crime. It should be.

CONVICT CRIMINOLOGY

Example: Richards and Ross (2002)

Convict criminology stems from the first years of the twenty-first century in the USA and has grown with increasing momentum over the past decade. Led by former prisoners who have gained academic credentials and qualifications, convict criminology takes a critical approach to the criminal justice system and penal expansion and seeks to add a grounded voice to debates on crime. In particular, its adherents seek to challenge traditional understandings of crime, the penal system, prisoners and former prisoners and how such matters are conceptualized, represented and discussed. Importantly, convict criminology approaches existing practices, research and political commentary with a critical lens focused through personal experiences.

Central to its objective is the relevance of our personal experiences of the criminal justice/penal system and criminal justice theorising and policy development. Convict criminologists advocate the need for critical and 'insider' perspectives criminological research generated from personal experiences of the CJS, and thus many, though not all have convict criminologists have themselves once been offenders. Convict criminologist argue that criminology as a subject stands to benefit from the more structured development and inclusion of academic accounts generated by prisoners and ex-prisoners. In 2001, Stephen Richards and Jeffrey Ross published their 'manifesto', 'The New School of Convict Criminology', in the journal *Social Justice*. This was followed shortly afterwards with a co-edited collection of essays, *Convict Criminology* (Richards and Ross, 2002), establishing their perspective and methods. In the UK, convict criminology is now emerging as a unique and separate perspective, and will likely develop more in coming years.

Key points of convict criminology

- Experience of the criminal justice system and experience of incarceration can be unique and can offer new perspectives on crime and criminalization.
- Convict criminology approaches existing practices, research and political commentary with a critical lens focused through personal experiences.

POSTMODERN AND LATE-MODERN CRIMINOLOGY

Examples: Henry and Milovanovic (1996), Young (2007)

Postmodernism has been a much used term in the social sciences, with its debates and ideas proving useful to criminologists. However, unfortunately, due to the complexity of terminology used in the writing, 'postmodernism' is often heavy and obscure and it is extremely difficult for students to get to grips with.

The key ideas are, however, really quite straightforward, and once learned will be useful for the whole of the period of study. There is not a postmodernist school of criminology as such, rather a large number of contemporary theorists frame their analysis and work in such a way that knowledge of these notions and ideas is important.

Essentially, the idea of postmodernity involves the notion that we live in an epoch that is different from a previous time period, which we term the 'modernity'. A good starting point, therefore, must be to identify what is meant by the term modernity. Modernity is a term used to describe the development of a secular rational tradition which had its origins in the seventeenth century's scientific revolution and the Enlightenment of the eighteenth century. The prestige of this European tradition and of the associated values of the Enlightenment in the twentieth century has depended crucially on the worldwide success of science and technology. It is this success that has projected the European tradition far beyond the Western world. The principal features that may be seen to characterize the idea of modern society can be identified in three main areas – economic, political and cultural.

Economically, modernity involved the development of the capitalistic practices of a market economy. It involved the growth of production for profit, rather than immediate local use. Politically, modernity involved the consolidation of the centralized nation state and the extension of bureaucratic forms of administration, systematic forms of surveillance and control and the development of representative democracy and political party systems.

Culturally, modernity involved a challenge to tradition in the name of rationality and stressed the virtues of scientific and technical knowledge. Hence one suggestion is that modernity is characterized by moral certainty. There is a confidence and belief in the superiority and infallibility of natural science which filtered through into the social sciences, and in particular to social and political theory. Thus, it has been argued that a characteristic of modernity was a confidence in the explanatory power of grand theories to solve the problems of humanity.

In contrast, postmodernity is a term used to describe the state after modernity, and the challenge to the secular scientific tradition. In some ways it could be seen as a call to abandon 'grand' theory of the social sciences or rational scientific human progress, especially in the post-Second World War world where ideologies of Communism and National Socialism seemed to

have led only to totalitarianism, world war and holocaust, and the technological ability for human beings to destroy themselves on a massive scale
(e.g. the nuclear bomb).

Very simply put, then, the idea of the postmodern involves claims that
modernist features of society are being challenged, and underlying these
changes was the beginning of an economic and political transformation.

Importantly, there are a number of ideas associated with postmodernism.
For example, 'post-Fordism' is a term used to describe how traditional,
production-based manufacturing in developed Western countries gave way
to a service industry. Primary production was displaced by secondary exploitation (especially of science and technology) and consumers outshone pro-
ducers in the economy, where old categories of analysis such as class seemed
to make little sense and so the intellectual categories around which modernist thinking was framed, lost resonance. Hence we have seen a move from
mass production-line technology towards flexible working patterns and a
flexible labour force. This in turn involves a weakening of trade unions,
greater reliance on peripheral and secondary labour markets, the development of a low-paid and part-time, often female, labour force, and the shift
towards a service, rather than manufacturing, economy. On the side of capital owning and controlling interests, it involves a greater stress on enterprise
and entrepreneurialism, corporate restructuring and the growth of small
businesses acting as subcontractors to larger firms. Hence the system of
social life in countries such as Britain and the US is much changed to that
which existed in the 1920s and 1930s.

Another term that you may encounter in criminology associated with the
changes suggested above is 'neoliberalism'. Essentially this term is used to
describe free market ideas, such as those promoted by the British Prime
Minister, Margaret Thatcher, and the US President, Ronald Reagan. These
included the offering of tax cuts as a means to facilitating consumer choice,
the dismantling of elaborate state planning and provision in the fields of welfare, and the rolling back of the state so as to facilitate economic liberalization,
free trade and open markets. Neoliberalism supports the privatization of
nationalized industries, deregulation, and enhancing the role of the private
sector in modern society.

So, postmodernity is an ambiguous term, but it is often used as shorthand
to describe an uncertain period. But it is not simply a period of uncertainty. It
is a period of different discourses (scientific, religious, political, etc.) each of

which might be right for different people in different contexts, and this cultural impact of postmodernity has become the basis of a whole school of social theory. However, at the heart of this notion are ideas about human diversity and social transformation and social fragmentation, where the end outcome is not clear. For example, the fragmentation of social institutions such as class and status may increase our uncertainty in our knowledge of how we understand society. However, the same trends also allow for liberation and the expression of the diversity of human needs, interests and sensitivities.

However, there is potentially a 'dark side' to postmodernism. If there is no such thing as 'truth' how does one provide an argument for anything? Is everything simply subjective? Are all viewpoints of equal merit? What foundations are there for criminology if the criminal law is to be seen simply as subjective and relative? The relativism implied by postmodernism denies the possibility of truth, and hence of justice, in anything other than a purely subjective form. Crime and the identification of harm are categories constituted by the discourse but they are, nevertheless, 'real' in their consequences. Surely some positions must be privileged – for example, if no ideology holds true, then how do we understand the fact that if we are diagnosed with cancer we have a better survival chance with chemotherapy or radiotherapy than being treated by a New Age healer using crystals?

It is in part as a reaction to that recognition that a contrasting term, 'late modernity', is proving increasingly common in academic texts. As a concept it essentially describes the idea that the condition in some highly-developed present-day societies is that of a continuation or development of modernity, rather than as a distinct new state, postmodernity. Whereas adherents of postmodernity presume the ending of the modernization process and the dawning of a new era, those who talk of late modernity argue that it involves a continuation or even a radicalization of the modernization process, demonstrated in technological and social transformations. Contemporary societies are thus a clear continuation of modern institutional transitions and cultural developments. Late modern theorist criminologists such as Jock Young tend to see society as characterized by complex, global capitalist economies and a shift from state support and welfare to the privatization of services where the prevailing mood of the times could be said to be vertigo, a term used to capture and characterize a society filled with anxiety, inequality and division (Young, 2007).

Key points of postmodern and late modern criminology

- Postmodernity signifies a break with modernity and the decline of grand theory.
- The contemporary period is a markedly different phase, with a plurality of competing and complementary ideas.
- Social, economic and cultural changes from the period of modernity must be recognized in the criminological project.

COMPARATIVE CRIMINOLOGY

Example: James Sheptycki and Ali Wardak (2005)

Comparative criminology considers changes since the end of the Second World War, but tends to focus on processes of economic globalization abetted by better international transportation and ease of communication, which have provided new opportunities for international criminal activity. Essentially comparative criminology is something of a catch-all term that unites a diverse body of writing which shares in common a concern with cross-cultural perspectives on a broad range of topics related to crime. Thus comparative criminology is not really new; indeed, Hermann Mannheim, one of Britain's first criminologists, used the term in the 1950s. However, a renewed commitment to comparative and international criminology has emerged as a result of the implications of globalization and the seeming punitive turn that appears to be more or less global in scale. For that reason, many comparative criminologists suggest pursuit of a criminological perspective that allows and facilitates criminologists to examine practices worldwide with a concern with global justice. Indeed, advocates of comparative criminology often follow a critical perspective and argue that comparative criminology should be engaged with issues of global injustice, insecurity and harm. Comparative criminologists therefore seek to ask questions such as: how far does it still make sense to distinguish nation states, for example in comparing prison rates? Is globalization best treated as an inevitable trend or as an interactive process? How can globalization's effects on space and borders be conceptualized?

> ## Key points of comparative criminology
>
> - Comparative criminology is something of a catch-all term that unites a diverse body of writing which shares in common a concern with cross-cultural perspective on a broad range of topics related to crime.
> - Globalization and new technology have created new opportunities for crime, rendering traditional boundaries and borders less rigid.
> - Criminal justice policy and practices transfer across boundaries and borders.
> - Criminologists should seek to examine practices worldwide with a concern with global justice.

PSYCHOSOCIAL CRIMINOLOGY

Example: Gadd and Jefferson (2007)

Psychosocial criminology essentially describes an emergent strand of theorizing that draws on both traditional sociological theorizing and psychoanalytic theory. In the 1990s, a renewed interest in a psychosocial perspective developed in criminology, suggested initially in relation to masculinity theories and works on 'fear of crime'. The later part of this work suggested that in order to understand fears about victimization, criminologists needed to look at how life events and anxiety levels produce differential fear of crime not along simple age or gender lines, but linked to people's individual biography and background. In truth, rather than being founded on Freudian theory, psychosocial criminology owes more to a variant on Freud's work developed by Melanie Klein. Klein pursued one of Freud's suggestions, arguing that crime might arise from *excessive guilt* rather than lack of a conscience, and therefore those who employ psychosocial criminology tend to endorse life history events within individual offenders. Therefore psychosocial criminology is associated with a revival of interest in offenders' biographies and inner, sometimes unconscious, emotional experiences, and with the importance of emotion as a source of understanding of crime. Methodologically, understanding of these is arrived at through a blend of life history interviewing that sometimes uses a technique termed free association narrative interviews (FANI), which uses questions that persuade interviewees to remember specific events. The aim and principle of free association is based on the idea that it is the unconsciously motivated links between these events and people's thought processes that provide insight into the emotional meanings of interviewees' accounts. Therefore uncovering sometimes unconscious or unrecognized motives is at the heart of this process. Indeed Gadd and Farrall have argued that when it comes to crime:

> The latent or unconscious meanings embedded in offenders' narratives are as important as the actual words, narratives or discourses used. These unconscious meanings can only be 'got at' through in-depth interpretive work. (Gadd and Farrall, 2004: 148)

Psychosocial approaches therefore are interpretative and based on the criminologist making judgements about offender motivation, but doing this while taking into account the social context of crime. Such psychosocial methods have been employed to assist in understanding of a range of types of offending, on topics such as domestic abuse, masculinities and crime, racial harassment, offender motivation and desistance from crime. However, there may be some problems with such an interpretive framework where the criminological academic projects judgements about an individual's unconscious motivations for crime, and with traditional psychoanalysis, which was based largely on untestable theorizing. However, as a response to such criticisms this psychosocial work has also incorporated an element of sociological theorizing that recognizes the importance of disadvantage, social marginalization and social inequality as important factors that affect such individual psychic practices, and should not simply be equated with a simple reprisal of past, psychoanalytic ideas wholesale.

Key points of psychosocial criminology

- Criminology must return to questions about motivation and seek to understand the behaviour of individual offenders.
- Such understanding is likely generated through an interplay of psychoanalytic concepts and sociological theory.
- There may be hidden, unconscious drivers of crime rooted in individual biographies.

CRIME SCIENCE

Key thinkers: Laycock (2005), Tilley and Laycock (2007)

Crime science is the study of crime in order to find ways to prevent it. Three features distinguish crime science from criminology: it is single-minded about cutting crime, rather than studying it for its own sake; accordingly it focuses on crime rather than the offender; and it is multidisciplinary, notably recruiting scientific methodology rather than relying on social theory. Crime science was conceived by the British broadcaster Nick Ross in the late 1990s, working in collaboration with the Metropolitan Police and Professor Ken Pease as a deliberate departure from criminology, which was perceived as overly sociological (and often politicized). The main proponents are now mainly located in the Jill Dando Institute of Crime Science (JDI) at University College London, established in 2001 and named in tribute to the murdered BBC television colleague of Ross. The institute was established in the Engineering Sciences Faculty, and has ties to the physical sciences (such as physics and chemistry) but is multidisciplinary and drawing on fields such as statistics, environmental design, psychology, forensics and geography.

Crime scientists seek to cut crime rates, and are often keen to predict and promote ways in which to aid detection. It is therefore very interested in application and practice. However, in this way it often asks few questions about the socio-economic and political responses to crime and therefore, for some critics, is in its worst manifestations simply apologist and endorsing of state exercise of power. Yet crime scientists would counter that with the claim that they seek to reduce victimization and work to cut crime rates for the civic good.

Key points of crime science

- Criminologists should seek practical scientific criminology that looks to provide effective improvements that prevent crime, or aid in the detection of those who perpetrate it.
- Criminology should not be unduly theoretical or concerned with conceptual issues; it should be complementary and work with traditionally non-associated science subjects, such as chemistry, engineering, geography to aid in designing out crime or capturing criminals.

Remember – Influential criminologist Sir Leon Radzinowicz expressed a concern with the divide between criminological theory and policy and practice in Britain: 'What I find profoundly disturbing is the gap between criminology and criminal policy' (1999: 469). Do you think his appraisal is correct with regard to contemporary criminological theory?

While Radzinowicz is quoted a little out of context here, the argument that criminological theory has less influence upon contemporary debate is one that could be fiercely contested. Three strands of theory have proved extremely influential in recent years in Britain: right realism, left realism, and administrative criminology. I would expect a good student to know about these theories, to be able to summarize them, but also to be able to demonstrate how they have influenced policy development; for example, administrative criminology has links to situational crime prevention, while right realism has influenced the development of 'zero tolerance' styles of policing.

Further resources

I have called this chapter 'Contemporary criminology' because it intends to highlight some of criminology's emerging theoretical positions. That stated, what in criminology counts as contemporary is changeable, and new insights and contributions are always emerging. The best way to stay aware of developments in criminology is through journals: the *British Journal of Criminology, Theoretical Criminology, Criminology and Criminal Justice*, the *European Journal of Criminology* and the *Howard Journal of Criminal Justice* are all valuable and should not be overlooked as sources of information, with a number offering favourable subscription rates to students. Similarly, the Centre for Crime and Justice Studies, at Kings College, London offers discount joining rates to students. Members receive the centre's magazine *Criminal Justice Matters*, a quarterly publication (each on a specific theme) that blends theoretical academic criminology with practice issues, and will assist in maintaining awareness of contemporary concerns within criminology.

Much of the work by core thinkers highlighted above is new and recent, and students should read the works of the core authors which will be widely available to get a feel for the contemporary developments in the discipline as they are often not well summarized in some of the more established criminology textbooks. Beyond this Muncie, Talbot and Walters edited collection *Crime: Local and Global* (2009) is an excellent additional text for expanding on some of the emergent areas outlined above including cultural, green and comparative criminology.

2.6   CRIME STATISTICS AND CRIME DATA

RUNNING THEMES

Crime statistics and crime data are sources which have been used by a wide number of criminologists from a range of perspectives, yet as with the **research methods** that inform their collection, they have been much criticized. Crime statistics have a **practical application** and can influence both policy and practice in the criminal justice system. Whilst they can present a picture of rates of crime and victimization, they also **discriminate** against some groups. Much of the problem with crime statistics arises out of concerns about **evidence** (in terms of how accurate a picture of crime they can give us). Do they present an accurate **representation** of the people's experiences or levels of crime or the amount of crime in society?

KEY THINKER

Adolphe Quetelet (1796–1874) Quetelet was a Belgian astronomer who came across the first French crime statistics whilst working in Paris. After noticing that deaths year on year were consistent, he suggested that correlations in this social data were similar to those consistencies found in astronomy. As Quetelet studied crime statistics in greater detail, he formed the opinion that some people were disproportionately more likely to commit crime than others; these people tended to be young, male, poor, unemployed and under-educated. Quetelet eventually suggested that propensity to engage in crime was due to moral character, and that instilling 'rational and temperate habits, more regulated passions and foresight' would prevent crime. The logical solution to him lay in enhancing 'moral education', improving social conditions and increasing the quality of individuals' lives. Crime was not freely chosen but was dependent upon and even created by society.

THE DEVELOPMENT OF CRIME STATISTICS

Crime statistics are essentially one of the criminologist's main tools in investigating 'crime levels', 'patterns of crime' and 'crime trends'. As a subject, criminology is reliant upon evidence, and crime statistics or data are often the basis of criminological theory. The government in France in 1827 published the first crime statistics. It was shortly after this that Andre-Michel Guerry (1802–66) and Adolphe Quetelet (see above) published perhaps what could be regarded as the first works of scientific criminology by using these statistics. This began a trend of positivistic criminology that attempted to make assertions about crime based upon statistical information.

Primary and secondary data in criminology

To recap from Chapter 2.2 on research methods, social scientists interpret those terms in a manner that is different to historians. Primary data to the social scientist is data that they themselves have collected. A variety of different research methods may have been used to collect this data, for example

(Continued)

(Continued)

interviews, questionnaires and observations. A secondary source is information that has been produced by someone else, but a social scientist uses for his or her own purposes. Secondary sources will therefore contain any biases or faults that were built into the original work. This is extremely important when we look at criminological work that is based upon crime statistics, as bias or inaccuracy built into data collection will impact upon findings.

Crime statistics have a political application in that they are used by people, often to further or support their arguments and assertions. Crime statistics can be abused, and are always open to interpretation. You must ask questions whenever someone attempts to make claims that they suggest are supported or even 'proved' by crime statistics.

RECORDED CRIME AND OFFICIAL STATISTICS

Each year the Home Office and various other governmental departments will produce a mass of statistics, many of which are potentially valuable to criminologists. The most obvious example of this data for the criminologist is criminal statistics, but others including prison statistics and social trends are also of great use. These statistics can now be accessed fairly easily through the internet, and you might be well advised to familiarize yourself with some of this information. In England and Wales, official crime data gathered from police and court records dates back to 1876, and despite warnings to the contrary, have also long been treated as an accurate measure of crime (especially by both the media and politicians). Official crime statistics essentially deal with all recorded crime (generated through police records).

There are a number of problems with this information, however; perhaps the obvious starting point is with the victim reporting the crime, which we know to be one of the core problems with official crime statistics. As official statistics only record *reported* crime, the victim must decide to report the crime to the police if the crime is to be recorded. There may be a number of instant barriers that prevent this from happening: the belief that police won't be able to do anything; the victim regarding the matter as too trivial; fearing the consequences of reporting; not wanting to get involved with the police; a lack of respect for the police; or feeling embarrassed or ashamed. It is estimated that there is massive under-reporting of crime. Anything up to 50 per cent of crime is therefore not evident in official crime statistics. Criminologists term this unreported crime 'the dark figure'.

If the victim *does* contact the police, there is still no guarantee that the crime will be recorded. The police have to decide whether what is reported to them amounts to a crime, and it may be that what the victim regards as an offence may not be viewed by the police as a breach of the criminal law. If that were to be the case, the police would not record the incident. If the police believe that a crime has been committed, the police then have to decide if it is a 'notifiable offence'. The meaning of this term and the crimes that it covers are detailed in the rules regarding which crimes are counted, produced by the Home Office.

The crimes that are recorded can change and vary. Clearly such changes do raise questions about what general inferences can be made about accurately comparing levels of crime and crime trends for different times.

Many introductory criminology and criminal justice courses contain assessment and exam questions on crime statistics and crime data, with questions about the reliability of official crime statistics commonplace. Remember such questions almost naturally lend themselves to critical analysis (see Part 3).

CRIME 'CLEAR UP' RATES

Included in official crime statistics are details of how many crimes are 'cleared up' and details of the number of people who are 'preceded against'. However, here again official statistics can only give a partial picture. The Home Office governs the rules regarding the circumstances in which a crime can be regarded as cleared up. The most common refers to when a person has been 'proceeded against' for an offence, which means that some type of formal action has been taken, for example, the perpetrator has received a police caution. However, this also includes being taken to court but not subsequently convicted. A crime can also be regarded as cleared up if a court takes it into consideration (essentially if the individual admits the offence but is not sentenced specifically for it). Crimes can also be regarded as cleared up if the individual admits the offence but it is thought that there would be no useful purpose in prosecuting that individual.

Common pitfall

Do not take 'proceeded against' to mean that the crime has necessarily been solved, as this is not the case.

It is this that in the past has caused a great deal of controversy, in particular relating to a police practice known as 'cuffing' where known offenders, often already in prison, helped the police to improve clear up rates by admitting to crimes that they had not committed or had no knowledge of.

That stated, clear up rates overall are very low: the 2003–4 crime statistics showed that the proportion of recorded crimes that were detected through an offender being charged or summoned, cautioned, having an offence taken into consideration or receiving a fixed penalty notice was just 18.8 per cent, a fall from nearer 50 per cent in the 1960s. There were 4.3 million offences recorded by the police in 2009–10 and only 1.2 million crimes resulted in sanctioned detections. (Sanctioned detections are those where the offender receives some formal sanction, such as being charged or summonsed, cautioned, reprimanded or given a final warning.) However, there are also large differences in the clear up rates between different types of crime, with the most serious categories of crime generally having the higher clear up rates than property offences. For example, detection rates are lower for crimes such as offences against vehicles, where the offence generally only comes to light some time after it has been committed and the offender has left the scene, but high for drug offences which tend to occur when a police officer stops and finds someone in possession and takes some form of immediate action.

THE ADVANTAGES OF USING OFFICIAL CRIME STATISTICS

Whilst there are clearly limitations in using crime statistics, criminologists generally tend to highlight the problems, and not address some of the advantages of statistics. The principal issue has to be that if one isn't going to use crime statistics to make inferences about the extent of crime in society, what else can be used? The answer is that there is little. Both official crime statistics and the

British Crime Survey are well resourced, and there would be little opportunity for independent researchers to undertake such extensive analysis. The government routinely collects data that researchers would otherwise undoubtedly find it difficult to access. Similarly, the ethical complexities involved in the research process generally are removed when a researcher uses secondary data, such as crime statistics. If the researcher recognizes the bias and problems that are inherent in the data, crime statistics can provide at the least a useful starting point for criminologists.

Although crime statistics are often heavily criticized, there is certainly an argument to be made for the usefulness of this data. We must ask ourselves, if we totally discredit crime statistics, as a means of knowing about the extent of crime, is there an alternative source that could tell us more?

'MEASURING THE DARK FIGURE'

The British Crime Survey (BCS)(renamed the Crime Survey for England and Wales in 2012)

During the 1960s, the 'dark figure of crime' ignored by official statistics came to be scrutinized by a number of American studies. Experimental surveys were carried out with random samples, where households were asked whether anyone in that property had been the victim of crime within the previous year, and whether this offence had been reported to the police. These surveys are now referred to by criminologists as 'victim surveys', with the best known of these being what was formerly called the official British Crime Survey (BCS). (As of 2012 it has been renamed the Crime Survey for England and Wales.) This survey, conducted annually by the Home Office, is now cited as a much more reliable picture of the true extent of crime than police statistics, because it asks a random section of the population about their experience of crime in the previous 12 months, and therefore bypasses some of the criticisms of official statistics stemming from the problems with recording crime. The complex sampling procedure used to generate it aims to produce a representative picture of cross sections of all private households in England and Wales, and all individuals aged 16 or over living in them.

However, there are a number of problems with this survey. As it draws evidence from the public, it is somewhat subjective, and the crimes that are reported are not always easily classifiable (which makes comparisons with police records difficult). As it only surveys households it makes no mention of crimes committed against business premises (commercial burglaries, shop thefts) and excludes homeless people, who are victims of a disproportionate amount of crime. Similarly the exclusion of those under 16 may also lead to exclusion of some types of offence (robberies involving mobile phones are most prevalent amongst young people). As the individual needs to know that they were a victim, it can also miss complex frauds and what criminologists term 'corporate' and 'white-collar' crime. There have also been a number of questions raised regarding the accuracy of self-reporting, with the potential for exaggeration, forgetfulness, unwillingness to disclose, and misunderstanding, all potentially serving as limiting factors. That stated, despite potential limitations, historically the BCS has been regarded by many criminologists as a much more accurate picture than that provided by official statistics.

Local crime surveys

Whilst the British Crime Survey is now regarded as presenting a much more accurate picture of the extent of crime than official statistics, it tells little of the specific geography of crime. In particular it allows little insight into the experiences of urban 'high crime' estates. This factor was recognized by left realist criminologists, who emerged in the 1980s, and who argued that rises in crime were real, and were felt most by those in deprived inner city estates.

A number of criminologists of the left realist school decided to study crime in specific areas, and sought to use victim surveys to explore the experience of crime in both Merseyside (Kinsey, 1985) and Islington (Jones, MacLean and Young, 1986). These studies supported the assertions of their authors regarding the damaging effects of crime on particularly poor neighbourhoods, and displayed much higher levels of crime than official statistics. The studies were not without problems with regard to their research methods, but highlighted a number of features previously not seen in official studies.

FEMINIST VICTIM SURVEYS

Whilst the studies undertaken in Merseyside and Islington are somewhat different to the BCS, in that they attempted to present a less distorted picture of crime, and the left realists made advances in documenting the lived experiences of some marginalized groups, the picture presented would be distorted if the achievement were to be credited to them alone. In the 1980s, the desire to learn more about the lived experiences of crime for the very poor, ethnic minorities and women influenced left-leaning local authorities to fund research. Whilst that helped the left realist causes, it also allowed feminist criminologists to begin to investigate women's experiences of crime, and reinforced the stark reality that it is 'the home that is the place where women are most likely to be sexually or physically assaulted' (Stanko, 1998: 41). This point was perhaps made most strikingly by Hammer and Saunders (1984), who interviewed 129 women in Leeds to gain insight into their experiences of crime. They found that 59 per cent of the sample had experienced either sexual harassment, the threat of sexual violence or actual sexual violence within the previous 12 months. They also found that there were four reported cases of serious sexual assault, which was more than the 1982 BCS found in some 11,000 interviews!

THE OFFENDING, CRIME AND JUSTICE SURVEY

The Offending, Crime and Justice Survey (OCJS) (also known as the Crime and Justice Survey), is the first national longitudinal, self-report offending survey for England and Wales. The first OCJS began in 2003 (and also repeated in 2004, 2005 and 2006) after being commissioned by the Home Office. The survey was developed in response to a significant gap in data on offending in the general population and some of the omissions of the BCS concerning the estimated crime rate with the BCS. A specific aim of the OCJS was to monitor trends in offending among young people. The sample of respondents was drawn from persons aged 10–25 years, resident in private households in England and Wales.

The OCJS provided measures of self-reported offending of individuals surveyed; indicators of repeat offending; trends in the prevalence of offending; and information on the nature of offences committed, such as the role of co-offenders and the relationship between perpetrators and victims. The OCJS also provides some information on the extent and nature of young people's personal victimization, something long omitted from the BCS.

The OCJS is therefore a similar victimization survey to the BCS. While the latter covers adult respondents aged 16–59 years only (apart from the occasional youth boost sample), OCJS respondents are younger (aged 10–25). Thus really each survey presents a complementary, but obviously different, picture of the crime-related experiences and circumstances of adults and young people. The BCS is also managed by the Home Office Research, Development and Statistics Directorate.

THE INTERNATIONAL CRIME VICTIMS SURVEY (ICVS)

Many countries have national victimization surveys. Yet often, attempts to use the data from these national surveys for international comparison have failed. Differences in definitions of crime and other methodological differences are too big for proper comparison; however, in 1989 a group of European criminologists started an international victimization study with the sole purpose to generate international comparative crime and victimization data. The project is now known as the International Crime Victims Survey (ICVS). After the first round, the surveys were repeated in 1992, 1996, and 2000 and 2004–05.

PROBLEMS WITH STATISTICS

As illustrated above, crime statistics can often throw up a range of findings that are quite frankly inaccurate and unrepresentative, here are some more examples:

- Victimization studies often show grossly low levels of serious interpersonal crime, such as the 1982 BCS which found only one attempted rape, a figure which for 11,000 interviews is simply nonsense.
- Self-report studies often display little variation in terms of juvenile delinquency between class and race, and considerably less variation between genders than can be expected. This has led some criminologists to suggest that there is no relationship between class and crime, a claim that again may not be the case in reality.
- The National Crime Victimization Survey (NCVS) in America has often shown white men to have a similar or greater likelihood of being assaulted than black men, which runs in total contradiction to homicide rates and other statistical evidence.
- The International Crime and Victimization Survey (ICVS) frequently reports rates of violence that are in total contradiction to homicide rates.

POLITICS AND CRIME STATISTICS

With each annual publication of the crime statistics, there will be an accompanying debate in broadsheet newspapers that can be extremely interesting. Editorials in broadsheet newspapers can provide insightful comment on what inferences crime statistics allow us to make, and these are usually accompanied by comment from the leading political parties.

Common pitfall

Crime and crime control is often a political business, and you should remember that while statistics are not necessarily politically driven, those who collect and use them may be. You should always approach statistical research with some caution, and be very careful not to fall into the trap of making arguments along the lines of 'the British Crime Surveys show that it is a fact that violent crime is rising'.

'How reliable are official crime statistics?'

This question really lends itself to using the advantages and disadvantages method as noted in Chapter 3.5, but remember to blend in some contemporary examples of the political debate that surrounds crime statistics. A good answer would display knowledge of the academic debate surrounding the use of official crime statistics. Mentioning Adolphe Quetelet and discussing the history of the development of crime statistics in brief could provide an opening for your answer, but don't neglect contemporary works (see the further resources below). Remember to be critical in your analysis, and credit both the positives and negatives associated with official crime statistics. Also remember that you should try to reach a conclusion.

Further resources

It is well worth remembering that Quetelet began writing on crime far earlier than Lombroso, but is not credited as the founding father of criminology. One of his assertions was that '[t]he Crimes which are annually committed seem to be a necessary result of our social organisation... Society prepares the crime, and the guilty are only the instruments by which it is executed'. In essence, Quetelet

(Continued)

(Continued)

was arguing that the causation of crime was not the individual, but features in society. It is therefore perhaps not surprising that politically, both Beccaria's notion of 'free will' and Lombroso's argument that the cause of crime was within the individual, found more lasting political influence. Recently there has been a great deal of criticism made of official crime statistics in books and journals by cultural criminologists (see as an example, Young, 2003) who have been very critical of administrative, positivistic criminology, and especially critical of statistical information.

Most good textbooks can provide further insight into discussion of crime statistics, but amongst the best is Tim Hope's chapter in Hale et al.'s *Criminology* (2009). There is a large amount of statistical information about crime now available on the internet. In Britain, the Home Office Research and Statistics Directorate website can be accessed through www.homeoffice.gov.uk, which also includes a link to the most recent British Crime Survey.

2.7 CRIME AND THE MEDIA

CORE AREAS

Media coverage of crime

The media and the fear of crime

Media news values

Theorizing the media and crime

Rethinking moral panics

Positive media representation?

RUNNING THEMES

Criminological discussion about the media tends to stress the **power** of the media, and its ability to **discriminate** and promote **inequality**. The media **representation** of crime is undoubtedly a very **political** process, which is driven by different **political** and **economic** motives, which in turn can impact upon public thinking about crime and influence political decisions.

KEY THINKERS

Leslie Wilkins introduced the concept of 'deviancy amplification' in his work *Social Deviancy* (1964). Essentially this idea describes a process where media, state and public reactions to non-conforming or deviant acts serve not to control the level of deviancy, but actually increase it. Wilkins' concept links with integrationist criminology and labelling theories.

Stan Cohen first published *Folk Devils and Moral Panics* in 1972 – a book which fits with the concepts of integrationist criminologists. In it, Cohen examines the construction of the 'Mods and Rockers' and introduced the notion of the 'moral panic'. The term 'moral panic' is one much used in sociology and criminology and still has contemporary relevance (examples include paedophiles, joyriders, football hooligans and mobile phone muggers) and it is vital to be familiar with Cohen's argument when debating media representation of crime.

MEDIA COVERAGE OF CRIME

Before we begin to look at just how the media uses crime, it may be valuable to consider how, when and why the media selects stories. Most media institutions seek to attract as wide an audience as possible to maximize their profits, and even media that is not profit driven has to compete with other forms that are for an audience. To attract and retain audiences media products have to entertain, be dramatic or exciting, and sometimes cause outright shock. It is on this basis that stories and features are selected by all forms of media. As crime is shocking, entertaining, dramatic and exciting, it is unsurprising that the media often chooses to use crime.

> In order to comment upon the media and crime, it is vital that you have knowledge of current issues and debates. To this end it is well worth reading both broadsheet and tabloid newspapers, and watching the media. It is also important to question what you are told by the media, for example ask yourself, 'Why is that headline being used?', 'Why is this news story appearing now?', 'Who is setting the agenda?', 'Whose opinion am I hearing?' and 'Is there another side to this argument?'

Studies into the media's use of crime would seemingly support the assertion that 'crime sells'. In 1989, in a study in the UK, a survey of ten national daily newspapers for four weeks between June and July found that, on average,

12.7 per cent of event-orientated reports were about crime (although there was a great deal of disparity between tabloid and broadsheet newspapers). If you conduct your own survey of either tabloid or broadsheet newspapers you will find that crime is a stable part of their reporting, as it is on television news. However, the types of crime that are reported are not representative. The crimes that are reported are shocking and alarming – murder, rape and serious violence. This can tend to convey the impression that such crimes are not rare (which they are) but are frequent, thereby creating an unrepresentative picture of the extent and type of crime prevalent in society.

THE MEDIA AND THE FEAR OF CRIME

Crime is seemingly a troubling aspect of life. That is perhaps unsurprising given that the word crime generally evokes a fear of the most serious criminal acts (murder, rape, serious violent assault). Yet these acts are relatively uncommon, whilst in reality we need to confront the possibility that many of those who commit offences are not that different to 'us'. Crime is not uncommon, but often it is not that extreme in nature.

However, fear of crime amongst the British is seemingly high. For criminologists an important issue is the public perception of the risk of crime, or 'the fear of crime'. The media is likely to play a central role in creating public perceptions of crime and therefore influencing their perceptions about the extent of crime and the risk of suffering it.

MEDIA NEWS VALUES

So how might the media contribute to society's understanding and perception of crime? A number of reasons have been suggested but there are perhaps two considerations that override all others:

1 **News value** – Events must meet a required level of significance to be perceived as 'newsworthy' that will differ according to the news medium (for example, whether the news medium is regional or national), and the location of the story (for example, a British serial killer who kills five people will receive considerably more attention than a large scale humanitarian disaster in a third world country). Similarly, once a story makes the press, it must continue to have an impact, something 'fresh'. As the process of criminal

investigation and prosecution can be timely, some stories may disappear only to be rediscovered at a later point (the murder trial at crown court some months later, for example).

2 **Impact** – The stories selected by the media are chosen for their impact. An element of shock may be enough, but essentially the main consideration is how the story will engage the audience. News editors will select stories that are sensational, with embellished descriptions. It is these stories that also seemingly have a large impact upon the public. Similarly, if the event is one which can generate a large swell of public sympathy, it will quickly be seized upon, for example, particularly violent physical assaults and robberies of the elderly are often lead stories in regional news reports. The crimes that receive the most attention are the crimes that happen least frequently, but are most shocking. Examples are the murder of James Bulger by two young boys in 1993, or the murders of Holly Wells and Jessica Chapman in 2002. Such crimes are extremely rare when compared to high frequency but less serious crimes that are unlikely to be reported in the media.

Highly graphic violent crime stories that contain sensational headlines not only seemingly have a massive receptive audience in the form of the general public, they also have an impact upon policy and practice in the criminal justice system. For example, the murder of James Bulger, mentioned above, is seen by a number of academics as kick-starting an unrelenting rise in the use of imprisonment. It also helped to overcome civil liberty arguments against the spread of CCTV, and was also influential in leading to the change in the common law presumption of '*doli incapax*', which presumed that children below the age of 14 did not know the difference between right and wrong – this then led to the age of criminal responsibility in the UK being reduced to ten.

But to see the media's role in creating a fear of crime solely through its reporting of 'real' crime is perhaps to underestimate the types of media that influence public opinion. Crime and the criminal justice system is a fascinating subject that interests a large number of people; yet it is also shrouded in mystery. Crime contains all the ingredients required to produce entertaining drama. It provides so much material for both fact and fiction accounts that are meant to entertain us, from novels to magazines, documentaries to soap operas. To suggest that the public are influenced only by the news media is perhaps to underestimate the way that popular culture can impact upon public perception.

THEORIZING THE MEDIA AND CRIME

Much discussion of the media's impact has been linked to integrationist criminology, for example, the media's role in labelling 'deviant' or criminal behaviours. When thinking about the way in which the media portrays crime, there are two theories which have remained extremely influential: deviancy amplification and moral panic.

There are two theorists who are synonymous with criminological theory linked to the media, both of whom have contributed primary criminological theories that seek to link the media with crime directly. These theories go some way toward addressing the way in which the media can understand their influence on the criminal justice process.

Deviancy amplification

British Criminologist Leslie Wilkins' concept of 'deviancy amplification' was developed and emerged at the height of the influence of interactionist criminology and 'labelling theories'. Wilkins suggested that deviancy amplification is a process whereby the media, police, public and political reaction to non-conformist behaviour acts not to control deviant behaviour, but has an opposite effect of increasing it. Wilkins used the term to explore the relationship between levels of tolerance and intolerance and the reinforcement of deviant identity. He suggested that in societies where there were intolerant responses to deviance, more acts were criminalized and more action taken against criminals. He suggested that this would increasingly lead to the isolation and alienation of groups who would therefore commit more crime, and be rejected more vehemently by wider society. As a result, a perpetuating cycle or 'positive feedback loop' would emerge. Wilkins therefore regards effective controls placed upon crime as increasing the levels of crime. The more effective the controls, the more marginalized the group, the more crime will be resultant. Whilst not empirically testable, the explanation still has some supporters (Silverman and Wilson (2002) draw upon it to explain the contemporary alarm over paedophiles). That said, Wilkins' concept has seemingly been surpassed by a theory that is still commonly used in criminology, that of the moral panic.

Moral panics

In what amounts to one of the seminal studies of criminology, youth, the media and social control, Stan Cohen presented a picture of the inter-relationships in the construction of deviance. Cohen argues that at times of wider social unease, or rapid change, folk devils and moral panics serve to create a sense of control over these events, groups and individuals who would appear to threaten the societal norms. His research was based upon the phenomenon of young people forming groups of 'Mods' and 'Rockers' in the 1960s and particularly their behaviour (which began with minor acts of vandalism and some violence in Clacton in Essex over the May bank holiday weekend of 1964) and the evolving social response that stemmed from this. The press printed oversensationalized stories of gang violence, and running battles as front-page news. This in turn led to increased policing of these groups, but also served to create a greater sense of being a 'Mod' or a 'Rocker' for young people, which polarized these groups even further. Together, these factors led in turn to more arrests, which served to justify the original reporting. Cohen suggested that there were three essential elements of control culture:

1 **Diffusion** – Which describes the process where events in other places and at other times may be connected to an initial event.
2 **Escalation** – Which describes the calls for action to counter a threat, for example, 'We shouldn't have to put up with their behaviour any more', or 'Something should be done'.
3 **Innovation** – Which details stronger powers that are granted to the courts or police to deal with the threat, for example, in the case of football hooliganism this could be the football banning order.

For Cohen, the media played a central role in publicizing the activities of the groups, and causing an accompanying uneasiness. He suggested that the media shape debate by providing further information, which then serves to reinforce the original reports.

The problems with the concept of the moral panic

In considering the role the media plays in socially constructing the public perception of crime and deviance, the moral panic thesis may be a useful one, but problems with it remain, for example:

• Not all 'folk devils' can be said to be vulnerable, or unfairly marginalized. Jewkes (2010) gives paedophiles as one such example, however other accounts see this group as 'demonized' and subject to a moral panic (Silverman and Wilson, 2002).

- The concept of the 'moral panic' fails to ask adequate questions about the initial causation of deviant behaviour. The term 'deviancy' attests to similarities between behaviours that are often different (is the fear of paedophiles comparable to the fear of recreational ecstasy use by young people?).
- According to Cohen's own testimony, moral panics should be short lived, however, there is some evidence that continual anxiety exists with regard to some forms of 'deviant behaviour'.
- There is a difficulty with the term 'morality'. Morality can imply a consensus view within society; however, whilst this may be true in some instances, other morals are not shared throughout society. Similarly we encounter problems when we consider that the term moral panic appears to have spread to embrace panics that contain 'little or no moral element' (Jewkes, 2010).
- Some accounts tend to see the moral panic as a tool of the political elite, where they cynically manipulate both the media and the public, whilst others see them as generated by the public in response to very real fears that exist; these accounts are at odds with each other.

RETHINKING MORAL PANICS

It can be easy to fall into the trap of displaying a superficial understanding of the term 'moral panic'. When you use this term, ensure that you are aware of some of the criticisms that can be made of it; while the idea might seem convincing, remember there are problems with this term.

It was not just Cohen's arguments that relied upon the notion of the moral panic, indeed the concept was central to Stuart Hall and colleagues' *Policing the Crisis* (1978), which suggested that the media seized upon mugging, and created an authoritarian-inspired moral panic. However, critics such as Waddington were extremely dismissive, indeed he noted that contrary to the arguments made by Hall and his associates, 'mugging' was undergoing real rises. He therefore questioned what a 'proportionate' response would be (1986). Taking this theme further there have been a number of accounts that have sought to reposition the notion of the moral panic. Goode and Ben-Yehuda (1994) have argued that the concept of the 'moral panic' needs to be revisited and have suggested that there should be three distinct theories or approaches to the moral panic:

1   **The grassroots model** – Which details the type of panic that is generated bottom up, where, for example, the public expresses a genuinely felt sense of concern about a threat, even if it is mistaken or misguided.
2   **The elite engineered approach** – Which is where a group of elites deliberately and consciously promote a concern or fear.
3   **The investment-group approach** – Which stems from the rule-makers and legislators, or the moral entrepreneurs who create moral panics in an attempt to create a crusade for greater control.

Goode and Ben-Yehuda (1994) also suggest that a moral panic has five core characteristics:

- a disproportionate reaction
- concern about a threat
- hostility toward the subject of the panic
- a widespread agreement that the threat is a real one
- volatility: moral panics are random in terms of scale or length.

POSITIVE MEDIA REPRESENTATION?

Much of the discourse on the media's representation of crime concerns whether it promotes a fear of crime – far fewer studies have suggested that the media can have a positive effect. Recently this position has been revisited slightly, with some academics even going so far as to suggest that the positive power of fictional portrayals of the criminal justice system can educate the public. For example, Wilson and O'Sullivan (2004) have argued that film and television drama can accurately represent the brutal realities of prison and be used to convey the message of prison reform. This is an interesting emerging debate that promotes the positive potential of media representations rather than accentuating the most negative media portrayals of crime and punishment.

"How useful is the concept of the moral panic in terms of examining the public's anxiety about crime?"

Questions on moral panics are somewhat of a given on criminology courses, however students often tend to tackle them by taking a similar descriptive route which deals with the main theoretical contributors. What is often missing is a more considered critique of the concept. In addition, it is worth considering concepts in light of recent developments and contemporary anxieties. Similarly, recognizing the plethora of media and the different ways these are used in different settings and forms by different groups is important.

Further resources

Recently criminologists have followed a lead from sociology and begun to discuss the notion of public criminology. More abstract uses of the term tend to relate to theoretical criminology and its engagement with policy, but if the subject is to be taken seriously by politicians and policy makers then criminologists must get better at engaging with the media. To that end, the criminologist David Wilson (2011) has written an interesting reflection on his role as a public criminologist that students might want to track down and read.

Yvonne Jewkes' (2010) *Media and Crime* is an excellent introductory textbook that presents extremely comprehensive coverage of this subject area, including up-to-date discussions, while Chris Greer's *Crime and Media: A Reader* (2009) is an excellent resource full of useful readings.

2.8   YOUTH AND CRIME

Core Areas

What's the trouble with kids today?

America: Chicago and juvenile delinquency

British studies of youth subcultures

Youth offending

Young people as victims

RUNNING THEMES

Young people are quite frequently the subject of debate about their criminality, and there is **evidence** to suggest that this is based in part upon **inequality** and **discrimination** – we tend to view youths as problematic, often because of their offending, but little consideration is given to their victimization. Young people themselves are a group whose voice is unlikely to be heard, and because they are relatively **powerless** in society, they tend to be frequently **represented** in a negative manner. Much criminology has attempted to examine the experiences of young people with this backdrop in mind, but clearly such discussion cannot be separated from interconnected subjects of **race**, **class** and **gender**.

KEY THINKERS

Geoffrey Pearson – Pearson's *Hooligan: A History of Respectable Fears* (1983) should be a starting point for you in putting contemporary 'adult' concerns about troublesome youth into perspective, both historically and sociologically. Pearson challenged the misconception that there existed a bygone 'golden era' in relation to young people's behaviour, arguing that many contemporary concerns, such as those regarding 'troublesome youth' were not new, but instead formed part of a long-established trend. Pearson was a notable figure at the National Deviancy Conference which was associated with the study of evolving youth subculture linked to 'interactionist' criminology (see for example, Cohen, 1972; Young, 1971) and he has long promoted the subcultural study of young people (Pearson, 1975).

WHAT'S THE TROUBLE WITH KIDS TODAY?

Fears about youth and criminality are nothing new, indeed, as Pearson has argued, there tends to be a perpetual concern regarding young people that is long established (Pearson, 1983). It is also difficult to separate the issue of youth crime into a unique subject area – as we have already seen, the question of youth frequently arises in accounts of the media and its reporting of crime. That stated, youthful criminality is a long-established area of study for criminology. This chapter does not seek to give an overview of the youth justice system, as there are plenty of books that do so, instead it looks specifically at what we know about youth crime, and explanations regarding youthful criminality that criminologists have presented.

Concern with youth, crime and the dangerous classes has not been restricted to contemporary British society; there has been an ever-present fear about youth and crime (particularly working class or poor youth and crime). There have been 'Teddy boys', 'Mods', 'Rockers', 'football hooligans', 'skinheads', 'joy-riders' and 'Chavs', the threat of youth crime is never distant – each generation has its dangerous young simply waiting to be discovered. Therefore it is perhaps unsurprising that many of the 'moral panics' we have encountered involve 'youth'.

> The concept of the moral panic (see Chapter 2.7) is inseparable from discussions on the topic of youth and crime. You would do well to remember that it is often media portrayals that influence public perceptions of problematic youth.

That stated, youthfulness is certainly a predictor of potential criminality. The peak age of offending for males is 18, whereas for females it is 15, and it is certainly true to suggest that the early onset of criminality is a very good predictor of the likelihood of a continual involvement in crime, as the vast majority of those who go on to be 'persistent' or 'career' criminals start to commit crimes in their early teens. Similarly, self-report studies also tend to suggest that offending can be fairly common amongst young people, with the Audit Commission report 'Misspent youth' estimating that the financial cost of youth crime to public services each year was around £1 billion. It has even been suggested that in reality, 'the youth crime problem is the crime problem' (Wilson and Ashton, 2001: 66). However, it is also worth stressing that while an estimated seven million offences are committed by under 18s each year, up to 85 per cent of young offenders cautioned don't come to the attention of the police again within two years, and while there is some disagreement whenever statistics are used, statistics seem to suggest that youth crime may have been falling for some years. Overall there were 176,511 proven offences by young people in 2010–11, down 11 per cent from 2009–10. In the last year there has been a notable reduction in offences by young people, in particular: motoring offences (24 per cent), breach of a statutory order (19 per cent) and theft offences (18 per cent). However, despite this decrease the estimated total cost to the country of police and justice for young offenders in 2007–8 was in the region of £4 billion annually.

AMERICA: CHICAGO AND JUVENILE DELINQUENCY

While in Britain academic inquiry into delinquency and youthful criminality tended to be linked to practical and policy concerns (and biological and psychological positivism) rather than a spirit of social inquiry, in America the agenda was different and enquiry was guided by scholarly endeavour. Particularly from the 1920s, investigations of juvenile criminality tended to stem from the pioneering sociological positivism and the early ethnographic work of the Chicago School of Sociology. Therefore American work on youth and crime did not have the same concern with promoting working practices. While sociologists did have a real impact upon political policy, this was perhaps less conscious and deliberate.

The Chicago School

- conducted 'ecological' research which aimed to understand the city of Chicago
- promoted qualitative methods – such as participant observation and life history
- undertook a number of studies with 'delinquent' youths
- promoted theories of social disorganization and cultural transmission
- proved to be influential in the development of theories such as strain and status frustration
- produced what are now regarded as classic studies of youthful criminality such as Clifford Shaw's *The Jack Roller* (1930).

Subcultural studies were first used by anthropologists in order to investigate the culture and practices of different societies, but were adapted and used by sociologists from the late 1920s to study social deviance. These studies were widely used by the 1950s in both Britain and America, especially by sociologists studying social deviance and juvenile delinquency, in order to argue that seemingly 'senseless' behaviour of such groups could be understood as a response to the problems that they faced. In both America and Britain, the influence of sociology as an academic discipline helped to promote the social disorganization theories and interactionist criminology, with attention focused upon youth crime (for some examples see Shaw and McKay, 1942; Cohen, 1955; Sykes and Matza, 1957; Cloward and Ohlin, 1960).

BRITISH STUDIES OF YOUTH SUBCULTURES

It is fair to suggest that in Britain the influence of subcultural studies such as those undertaken by the Chicago School were not influential until some years later, and academic discourse suggests that at this time British criminologists produced less ethnographic research into juvenile crime than their American counterparts. Perhaps this is partly due to the fact that there seems historically to be some difference in the types of gangs found in Britain and America.

In Britain, John Mays (1954) and David Downes (1966) were the first researchers to investigate youth delinquency in a manner similar to that of the Chicago sociologists. Momentum grew, as did studies of youth deviant subcultures, with the work of the Birmingham Centre for Contemporary Cultural Studies. Stuart Hall and Tony Jefferson's (1976) *Resistance Through Rituals* is a classic text that documents well the development of British youth subcultures, while numerous other studies conducted by the centre examined some aspects of youthful criminality. Indeed it was the subcultural study of youth that played such a substantial role in promoting interactionist, new deviancy and cultural forms of criminology.

YOUTH OFFENDING

Offending by young people is quite common. A 2006 survey found that 25 per cent of 11- to 16-year-old children sampled in a self-report servey in the UK admit to having broken the law in the previous 12 months (Philips and Chamberlain, 2006). However, the great majority of young people who commit offences do so infrequently. Similarly, the types of crimes committed by young people are rarely that serious, and are usually property crimes such as theft, handling stolen goods, burglary, fraud or forgery and criminal damage, making up more than two-thirds of all youth crime. Despite media attention on violent offending, few cautions or convictions relate to violence. After the peak age of offending, any criminal activity that young people are involved in usually declines, with a particularly sharp decline for criminal damage and violent offences. This is largely thought to be the effect of positive changes in young people's lives, personal and social development: completing education, gaining employment, leaving home and finding a partner can all lead young people away from crime. Where this cannot be said to be the case, however, is when young people have been in custody. The rates of re-offending for those in youth custody are far worse than those for adults. This may not simply be because prison for young people can be an incredibly traumatic and negative experience, but also because the vast majority of young people who appear in prison have experienced incredibly traumatic lives before prison; and this pattern is likely to continue after imprisonment. We also know that those young people who come into contact with the Youth Justice system are troubled and have often had difficult lives. For example, a study of young people in custody supervised by the Youth Justice Board has shown:

- 23 per cent reported that they had 'experienced abuse (i.e. physical, sexual, emotional, neglect)'. The figure for young people on detention training orders was 32 per cent, which compares with about 16 per cent of the general population of children. More females had experienced abuse compared with males (35 per cent compared with 20 per cent).
- 30 per cent had experienced 'significant bereavement'. This compared with 4 per cent of the general population of children who had experienced death of parent(s) and/or siblings.
- 12 per cent per cent had deliberately self harmed.
- 7 per cent had 'previously attempted suicide'.
- 25 per cent had 'any contact with, or referrals to, mental health services'. (Source Ministry of Justice Youth Justice Statistics 2010–11)

YOUNG PEOPLE AS VICTIMS

With some of the above points in mind it is perhaps a point well worth making that concern with youths as potential criminals has not been matched with a recognition or similar level of concern with youths as victims of crime. The perception of youths as troublesome has led to the belief that young people are criminals, rather than being victims. The alarming thing is that this is an inaccurate perception, quite simply because while crime is something associated with youth, so is victimization.

Youth victimization

In 2009, the charity Catch-22 published a report *Youth Victimisation – Actors not Victims* that undertook a review of the current policy and practice context as it relates primarily to children and young people growing up in England. It provides a useful overview synthesis of research on the extent of victimization of young people.

- Figures suggest young people experience almost twice the victimization risk of the population in general: findings from the 2005 Offending, Crime and Justice Survey (OCJS) showed

(Continued)

(Continued)

27 per cent of young people aged 10 to 25 as being the victims of personal theft or assault in the last year.

- Young people are more likely to suffer repeat victimization than other group. In the 2005 OCJS, 58 per cent of young people subject to assault without injury reported being victimized more than once within the last twelve months.
- In 40 per cent of cases the person committing the crime is known to the young victim and is most often a friend or sibling.
- Young people aged between 10 and 15 years are more likely to be victims of personal crime than young people aged from 16 to 25. Across both age groups (10–15 and 16–25) the most common form of victimization is assault without injury.
- Most incidents against 10 to 15 year olds happen at school, are perpetrated by other pupils or friends and are regarded by victims as 'something that happens' and 'wrong but not a crime'.
- Young people who have been excluded from school are more likely to be victims than non-excluded young people.
- Recent MORI data points to an increase in the proportion of young people who say that they have been threatened or physically attacked.

"In criminology, youth are frequently regarded as perpetrators, but infrequently viewed as victims. Discuss."

You should draw from the theories in this and other chapters to make an argument about the extent to which the representation of youth crime is accurate. Clearly, in many ways, youth is a factor that affects the likelihood of involvement in criminality, but our perception also comes from elsewhere. Remember that the concept of the moral panic might be useful in answering this question because it is possible to argue that our concern with youth crime stems from unjust portrayals in the media.

Further resources

As the subject of this book is 'theoretical criminology' rather than a more general analysis of the criminal justice system, this chapter has offered very little by means of introducing the specific differences in the treatment of young offenders. Students of criminology are well advised to seek some understanding of the separate nature of how the criminal justice system deals with young people who offend by looking further into the subject in relevant texts and textbooks

These who are new to criminology and want to expand their understanding of this area would be well advised to start with John Muncie's excellent *Youth and Crime* (2009).

2.9   GENDER AND CRIME

CORE AREAS

What do we mean by gender?

Feminist criminology

Criminology and women

Masculinities and crime

Crime as 'doing masculinity'

RUNNING THEMES

Clearly the subject of gender and crime is motivated by a desire to examine gender inequality, and therefore examine power relationships that characterize society, largely with a view to challenging **discrimination**. More recently feminist scholars have highlighted the need to also consider **race** and **class** along with **sex and gender,** motivated by an ideology that seeks to promote a socially just society.

KEY THINKERS

James Messerschmidt wrote *Masculinities and Crime* (1993), applying the concepts of 'hegemonic masculinity' to crime (the former being developed by sociologist Robert Connell who in turn was inspired by sociologist Gramsci). Hegemonic masculinity suggests that at any one point in time, there is a dominant form of masculinity (hegemonic masculinity) that subordinates all other forms of masculinity and femininity. Messerschmidt argued that many men's crimes are best understood as a means of 'doing gender' and making masculinity. Messerschmidt suggested that an understanding of various masculinities is central to developing an understanding of crime.

WHAT DO WE MEAN BY GENDER?

Before I go any further with this chapter it is important to clarify some of the terms that are used. In this chapter I talk about both sex and gender, and both of these are 'running themes' which you should keep in mind while you study the subject. However, it is important that you are clear on what is meant by these terms.

> Sex is a biological category and gender is a social construction – by this we mean that gender is different to sex. When we use the term 'sex', we talk about something which is biological and relatively fixed; when we talk about gender we accept social influences.

In order to demonstrate that gender differences *can* be explained by biology we would have to demonstrate that a substantial or universal difference between men's and women's roles exists across all societies and cultures, at all times and in all places. We would have to show that across all societies men adhere to one set of behaviours and women to another. Further, we would have to show that this difference could be attributed to biology rather than to different modes of upbringing. We know, however, that in many respects, women across time and cultures have inhabited many different worlds, so it is very difficult to sustain a view that biology is the reason for all differences between sexes and in gender roles.

Common pitfall

Many students tend to get confused when it comes to sex and gender and what the terms mean. It is important that you are clear about these terms.

FEMINIST CRIMINOLOGY

As you will now be aware there isn't a single 'feminist criminology' (see Chapter 2.4). Feminism tends to be associated with different theoretical perspectives. However, the divisions between feminist criminologies can be confusing, and at times serve to detract from the common concern of feminist thought, which shares some key traits regardless of the perspective it takes.

All feminist criminology:

- looks to highlight discrimination against women
- is concerned by male violence and oppression at both individual and societal levels
- focuses upon the unequal position of women in society, the victimization of women and women's victimization (including that perpetrated by the criminal justice system).

Liberal feminism

In criminology, liberal feminist work tends to assume that men and women are essentially the same, shunning notions of biological difference. It seeks to highlight the inequitable treatment of women and girls in the criminal justice system, and suggests that women are denied the opportunities that men are presented with, which include the opportunity to commit crime. Perhaps the greatest contribution of liberal feminism in criminology is the highlighting of the false claim criminology made of being gender-neutral, when the reality was that much criminology was gender-blind or based upon biological assumptions supported by no real evidence.

Radical feminism

Radical feminism advocates a more radical response to the experience of oppression that women encountered from both individual men and 'in social structures'. It seeks to analyse women's oppression and the structures that maintain it, but particularly focuses upon 'violence against women', 'sexual violence' and 'gender violence' as key strategies that are used to control women. Radical feminists also highlight the patriarchy of the criminal justice system. It has been influential in terms of activism that promoted organizations such as Women's Aid, the rape crisis federation. Radical feminism, as its name conveys, is more radical than liberal feminism, and aims to look at broader themes than individual oppression, instead seeking to understand the wider social circumstances that contribute to perceptions and understanding of crime. Therefore it is less concerned with individual experiences of oppression, and more concerned with the social conditions and structures that contribute to women's oppression.

Socialist feminism

Socialist feminism regards women's oppression as rooted in patriarchal capitalism, and argues that it is essential to consider the interplay between gender and class in order to understand crime. This position has been associated with male criminologists who declare themselves 'pro-feminist'. It occupies a different position from radical feminism insofar as it acknowledges the fact that much liberal feminism ignored issues of class. Rather than regarding patriarchy or men generally as the root cause of women's oppression, it predominantly looks toward capitalism to explain women's oppression.

CRIMINOLOGY AND WOMEN

Lombroso recognized that women are 'much less criminal than men' in general, and reasoned that this was due to women's unique biology. His work *The Female Offender*, written with William Ferrero, claimed that women's lesser criminality was explained by their 'piety, maternity, and want of passion, sexual coldness, weakness and underdeveloped intelligence' (1895: 151). Early Marxist criminologist Wilhelm Bonger suggested that 'the average woman of our time has less strength and courage than the average man, and consequently, commits on average fewer crimes than he' (1916: 472); whilst Otto Pollack (1950) is famous for his argument that women were biologically the 'weaker sex'. He asserted that women's criminality was potentially equal to that of men, however, women's ability to 'mask' their criminality (because of a deviousness that resulted from hiding menstruation and faking orgasm) meant that they were more likely to commit crimes typified by deceitfulness and concealment – such as thefts, shoplifting, and perjury. He also, however, argued that women could be influenced by men and were often accomplices rather than perpetrators. Similarly recognizing patriarchy in society, Pollack suggested that women could benefit from the 'chivalry' of male criminal justice practitioners, and therefore recognized social structures as influential. As criminology evolved, and control theories, functionalism and anomie, and labelling and interactions criminology became prominent, many criminologists tended to be stereotypically gender-blind.

> Remember that early criminology tended to make crude assumptions on the basis of biological myths. However, it would be naïve to assume that such crude ideas have disappeared entirely!

Second wave feminism emerged in the 1970s, and is often associated, for example, with the publication of Freda Adler's *Sisters in Crime* (1975). Adler argued that women's empowerment, as a result of the feminist movement during the 1970s, coincided with a dramatic rise in women's criminal activity. While women had made progress in the legal economy, 'a similar number of determined women have forced their way into the world of major crime such as white collar crime, murder and robbery' (1975: 252). It would be fair to suggest that Adler's theory proved controversial with other feminists. Carol Smart suggested that Adler had fallen victim to 'statistical illusions' (Smart, 1979) and as Pat Carlen suggested, Adler's new female criminal was a continuation of the 'maladjusted masculinity female' of traditional criminology, rejecting her proper feminine role (1983: 376–7).

Others, such as Kathleen Daly, have suggested, '[f]eminist perspectives in criminology are a very recent development, having only begun to appear in criminal justice and criminology texts in the early 1990s (Daly, 1994: 121). That stated, while feminist perspectives are a somewhat recent arrival, their influence has been substantial and has challenged the ideas of more traditional criminology (see Table 2.4).

Table 2.4

Traditional criminology:	*Feminist criminology:*
• was driven by biological assumptions created by male bias – men were superior, and there is a normal masculine and feminine type that can be linked with moral ideas • regarded female criminality as caused by biological factors and sexuality – for example, hormonal activities • linked women's offending to biological causes; criminal women were mad, bad, passive, and deceitful, or a combination of these factors • showed scant regard for women's experience as victims, only as offenders • was largely male-dominated and did not consider the male dominance in criminology or the criminal justice system worthy of investigation	• highlighted inequality and the double standards of morality – for example, the way in which women are sexualized but men are not • was keen to explore women's experiences in order to generate theories, particularly with regard to oppression, patriarchy and inequality • challenged the bias of traditional explanations of female criminality; highlighted the lack of appropriate attention given to women by criminologists • raised the prominence of women's status as victims of abuse, both physical and economic • emphasized the different social opportunities afforded to women because of male-dominated institutions and culture

MASCULINITIES AND CRIME

Crime is something that is male-dominated, whether involving property or violence, the powerless or the powerful, from petty property crime to multi-million pound fraud, crime is something that is predominantly done by men. In the 1990s, criminology turned its attention to a new question: 'Why is crime predominantly a male activity?'

For feminists, the answer was often found in the concept of patriarchy and all men having power over all women. Some male criminologists criticized this essentialism and the idea that all men could be placed in a universal category. They argued that men's experiences were different, and that men were divided and different in terms of the way that they enacted their masculine role. Therefore some social theorists introduced the concept of 'hegemonic masculinity', which is a notion suggesting that at any given time, a commonly accepted form of 'being male' that is dominant in society in gender terms, subordinates other forms of masculinity and femininity. This dominant or 'hegemonic' form of masculinity will be visible in ideas, values, images and customs in that society at that time.

CRIME AS 'DOING MASCULINITY'

Much of the work on masculinity and crime has been authored by men, but it should be noted that many of these men have aligned themselves with feminist criminology, declaring themselves pro-feminist. In general terms masculinity is a concept perhaps most prominently associated with sociologist Robert Connell (1987, 1995), who initially challenged the feminist notion of 'patriarchy', suggesting that such assertions failed to display an understanding of the multiplicity of maleness.

James Messerschmidt made Connell's work directly relevant to crime. Messerschmidt challenged the essentialism of some feminist writers – that is, the notion, for example, that 'all men are violent and all women victims'. Messerschmidt argued that the divide between genders is best understood by drawing upon three factors: the gender division of labour; and the gender relations of power; and sexuality. Messerschmidt argued that only by looking at these three elements, at one particular time, could we begin to understand how gender identities are created.

Messerschmidt noted that 'men use the resources at their disposal to communicate their experiences to others' – in other words, masculinity doesn't just exist, it has to be shown. It is in this show that 'for many men, crime serves as a "resource" for doing gender' (1993: 84). In other words, crime is one way that a man can show that he is a man.

"Why is crime predominantly the preserve of men?"

In answering this question you should be drawing upon the theories outlined in this chapter. Remember you can draw upon the notion of hegemonic masculinity proposed by Connell and furthered by Messerschmidt, but you could also draw upon some of the work of feminists. Also remember that biological explanations are relevant to these discussions and you might want to revisit that subject – do differences in biology explain differences in law breaking? Background facts such as the ratio of male to female in the prison population are useful to weave into your answer.

Further resources

Messerschmidt's *Masculinities and Crime* (1993) is still available, and you may find it useful in that it not only offers coverage of the issue of male crime, but provides an extremely worthy overview of 'traditional' criminology and feminist perspectives. You might want to think about what it might be that makes some crimes, such as football violence, almost uniquely male phenomena? An interesting recent account of the links between crime and masculinity and a fantastic example of criminological ethnography is provided in Simon Winlow's *Badfellas* (Winlow, 2001) which I would strongly recommend to students as an interesting and engaging text.

Most criminology textbooks will have a chapter on 'gender and crime' or 'women and crime', but can tend to neglect masculinity and crime as a subject area. Marisa Silvestri and Chris Crowther-Dowey's (2009) *Gender and Crime* brings together both feminist and masculinist perspectives, and is a good text. Karen Evans and Janet Jamieson's (2008) *Gender and Crime: A Reader* is also a useful source text.

2.10   RACE AND HATE CRIME

CORE AREAS

Race and hate crime

Race and the criminal justice system

Institutional racism in the CJS in the UK

Hate crime

RUNNING THEMES

Race is a core running theme, but in the power relationship between the offenders, the victim, the agencies of the state and the criminal justice system power and discrimination are central, as are issues such as inequality. Of course where race is concerned other issues such as gender, age and class also intersect.

KEY THINKERS

Ben Bowling studies crime, criminal justice, policing and community safety, but is perhaps notable as one of the UK's most prominent black criminologists. His early work was amongst the first to document the abuse, assault, and intimidation that was suffered by black and Asian people in Great Britain every day, using information gathered in an East London case study which then become his monograph, *Violent Racism: Victimisation Policing and Social Context* (1999). Bowling's work explains and analyses the process through which violence is targeted at these minorities, and looks at the failure of the police to respond to this problem, pre-empting many of the debates around hate crime. He also authored (with Coretta Phillips, 2002) *Racism, Crime and Justice*, and has been at the forefront in appealing for criminology to develop better understandings of minority perspectives.

RACE AND HATE CRIME

Criminology has long been attuned to the concepts of 'race' and ethnicity, which have been commonplace in empirical criminology since the first positivistic attempts to categorize offenders by physiological traits. Empirical and positivistic criminologists routinely use race and ethnicity as key socio-demographic variables to categorize and describe both offenders and victims of crime.

At the theoretical level, the topics of 'race' or ethnicity have infused many schools of criminological thought, from biological and social positivism, through Chicagoan sociology, to critical criminology and realist criminology. Unlike gender, which it is often held was historically neglected by criminologists, race and ethnicity were never so marginalized and have been present conceptually throughout the history of the discipline. In recent years, much of the focus of this empirical and theoretical attention has centred on official statistics, which reveal an overrepresentation of certain minorities among those arrested and imprisoned for some criminal offences.

However, in both the UK and the USA, debates over the years about 'race', ethnicity and society have been characterized by a tendency to take up polarized positions. For example, it has been suggested that the higher rates of conviction for black people are due to the fact that they are as a group more likely to commit crime, or because they are unfairly treated by the criminal justice system. More recently, victimology and concerns about crimes targeted against individuals because of some aspect of their identity has been the driving force behind the study of what are termed 'hate crimes', and under this heading academics have looked at how perpetration of crime can target individuals because of their race.

RACE AND THE CRIMINAL JUSTICE SYSTEM

What percentage of the UK's population come from ethnic minority backgrounds? According to the last census conducted in 2011, the ethnic make-up of the UK is predominantly white, with some 92.14 per cent of the population identifying themselves as white; with the majority (85.67 per cent of census respondents) identifying their ethnicity as white British. In all, black and minority ethnic (BME) groups constitute approximately 8 per cent of the population.

However, it is generally accepted that ethnic minorities, especially those of African, Caribbean and Asian origins, are at an increased risk of criminal victimization. The 2010–11 British Crime Survey (BCS) showed that the risk of being a victim of personal crime was higher for adults from a mixed background than for other ethnic groups. It was also higher for members of all BME groups than for white groups. Over the five-year period 2006–07 to 2010–11, there was a statistically significant fall in the risk of being a victim of personal crime for members of the white group of 0.8 per cent. The apparent decrease for those from BME groups was not statistically significant (i.e. it did not fall). Most alarmingly, black people in England and Wales were shown to be victims of murder more often. 11.8 white murder victims per million people, for black victims, that rate rises to 49.7, while for Asians it is just slightly higher than for whites at 18.3.

Levels of victimization do not give the full picture though, as members of the BME population are also subjected to targeted racist violence and hate crimes perpetrated against them. These patterns of higher rates of victimization are generally agreed upon, but how they are explained is more contested. Some academics suggest this is the result of white racism; others look to the socio-economic conditions; and others suggest that the blame might exist with the victims themselves.

Similar discussions exist concerning the way in which the criminal justice system treats some ethnic groups. Some – particularly those of African and Carribean origins – are much more likely to be stopped by the police and imprisoned by the courts. While conviction ratios for indictable offences were higher for white persons in 2010 than for those in the black and Asian groups (81 per cent for white, 74 per cent for black, and 77 per cent for Asian), a higher percentage of those in the BME groups who come before the courts are sentenced to immediate custody for indictable offences (white 23 per cent, black 27 per cent, Asian 29 per cent and other 42 per cent). In addition, on 30 June 2010, while the total prison population in England and Wales was 85,002, some 21,878 prisoners (just under 26 per cent) were from BME groups. Also, the most recent BCS has shown that by 2009–10, while there were decreases across the previous five years in the overall number of arrests and in arrests of white people, arrests of those in the black and Asian groups had increased. Black persons were stopped and searched 7.0 times more than white people in 2009–10. Again, this leads to debates about whether some ethnic minority members are more likely to commit crime than whites, and criminologists have variously addressed this issue in theories, in what has proven to be a divisive and controversial argument in both the UK and in the USA.

In early biological criminology this relation between race and crime was used to argue that certain racially defined populations were more prone to crime than others, and in turn as motivation for policies of social exclusion (from prohibition of mixed race marriage through social segregation) and also eugenic policies and genocide. Indeed, through the prism of the present it is easy to see the stark racism that is apparent in works such as those of Lombroso, who wrote of whole tribes and races more or less given to crime, citing Africans, Orientals, Gypsies and Jews as exemplars. Lombroso's work, *The Criminal Man* was not published in the USA until 1911, but still proved influential in the development of eugenicist policies.

Indeed, scientific racism has long been part of the criminal justice system, and this needs to be kept in mind when we consider the fact that, in some countries, crime rates vary significantly among racial groups, with some ethnic minority groups disproportionately represented in the criminal justice system. In both the USA and the UK, certain ethnic minority groups (in the USA, blacks and Hispanics; and in the UK, blacks and Asians) are disproportionately statistically represented at almost every stage of the criminal justice process and in every part of the criminal justice system (except as practitioners). However, most criminologists in both the USA and the UK would disagree with such a perspective and point to the continued evidence that the criminal justice system tends to discriminate against those from ethnic minority backgrounds at every stage of the process.

More recently, debates around race and crime have continued to produce controversy. For example, in 1994, Harvard psychologist Richard J. Herrnstein (who died before his book was published) and his co-author (and underclass theorist) Charles Murray published the extremely controversial book *The Bell Curve* (1994). Its central argument is that intelligence is substantially influenced by both inherited and environmental factors and is a better predictor of many personal dynamics, including financial income, employment, and involvement in crime than are an individual's parental socioeconomic status, or educational attainment level. The book also argues that those with high intelligence, the cognitive elite, were becoming separated from those of average and below-average intelligence, and that this is a dangerous social trend which is causing the United States to move toward a more divided society similar to that in Latin America. However, the controversy concerned the view that the authors were suggesting that black people were inherently inferior to whites in terms of intelligence, and the simplistic way in which they were linking low intelligence with activities such as crime, while paying scant attention to the socio-economic, political and cultural inequalities that had long led to immigrant groups being disproportionately represented in the criminal justice system. Indeed, Murray's underclass theory was also regarded as racist by some commentators, as it was clear that in relation to the United States the underclass could be conceived of as a 'black' problem, even if Murray denied this, and strongly refuted claims of racism when exporting his theory to the UK.

In contrast, but also in the context of the USA, Loïc Wacquant has argued a continuing lineage of social segregation on racial lines is entrenched within American practices of social control. Wacquant argues that it is possible to trace this through history through several phases, with several 'peculiar institutions' successively operating to define, confine, and control African-Americans in the

United States: slavery and the plantation economy from the colonial era to the Civil War; the Jim Crow system of legally enforced discrimination and segregation from cradle to grave which operated up to the Civil Rights revolution, which toppled it a full century after the abolition of slavery; the ghetto with the coming of industrialization and urbanization, from the early 1900s to the 1960s; and finally, through the carceral apparatus with mass imprisonment that saw one in three black males in the USA under some form of criminal justice supervision by the millennium. He suggests that slavery and mass imprisonment are genealogically linked and that one cannot understand the latter – its timing, composition, and smooth onset as well as the quiet ignorance or acceptance of its damaging effects on those it affects – without returning to the former as an historic starting point. Wacquant is therefore suggesting that a long entrenched form of racial prejudice serves as a core feature in social (and criminal justice) systems in the USA. However, other US criminologists have vehemently denied that the criminal justice system is racist. For example, in the USA, William Wilbanks, in his book *The Myth of a Racist Criminal Justice System* (1987), concluded that the criminal justice system is not racist because the evidence fails to prove that racism is present in all parts of the system during all steps of the criminal justice process. While there may be parallels between the USA and the UK in terms of long-standing, institutionalized practices of racism, the extent to which the two countries are comparable is debatable. However, the theme of racism as part of the criminal justice system is also recurrent in the UK.

INSTITUTIONAL RACISM IN THE CJS IN THE UK

The issue of racism in the criminal justice system was reignited after the murder of Stephen Lawrence, a black British teenager from Eltham, London, who was killed by a gang of white youths in a racist attack in April 1993. After the initial investigation, five suspects were arrested but not convicted. It was suggested that policing had failed in many aspects of the course of that investigation, but had specifically failed to deal with how the murder was racially motivated and that Lawrence was killed because he was black. Due to controversies involved in the case and perceptions that many aspects of the handling of the case by the police and Crown Prosecution Service were negatively affected by issues of race, the 'New' Labour government established a public inquiry. Held in 1998, it was headed by former high court judge Sir William Macpherson, and set out to examine the original Metropolitan Police Service (MPS) investigation. The inquiry concluded that the force was 'institutionally racist'. Specifically, Macpherson suggested that institutional racism should be defined as:

> The collective failure of an organisation to provide an appropriate and professional service to people because of their colour, culture, or ethnic origin. It can also be seen or detected in processes, attitudes and behaviour which amount to discrimination through unwitting prejudice, ignorance, thoughtlessness and racist stereotyping which disadvantage minority ethnic people (Macpherson, 1999, para. 0.34).

While institutional racism may help to explain, for example, the handling of the Lawrence case, or the death of Zahid Mubarek, another way racism may be apparent in the criminal justice system is in the level of employment of staff who are from BME backgrounds. In the UK in 2010, government figures suggested that the percentages of those from an ethnic minority background in the various parts of the criminal justice system were:

- 4.8 per cent of police
- 14.9 per cent of the Crown Prosecution Service
- 4.2 per cent of the judiciary
- 6.0 per cent of the National Offender Management Service (including the prison service)
- 14.1 per cent of the probation service.

Therefore, while the CPS and the probation service appeared to have the highest proportion of BME staff (of those considered), with more than 14 per cent of staff in each from a BME background, the police and the judiciary appeared to have the lowest proportions with fewer than 5 per cent from a BME group. While this number is closer to the number of the population who are of a BME background, it still suggests under representation in the criminal justice system. In addition, from government figures from 2010, about 96.6 per cent of senior police officers were white, while of the senior civil servants in the NOMS only one was from a BME background. This suggests that the striking under representation of people of BME origin in senior management positions may be a continuing feature of the criminal justice system, and perhaps also stands as further evidence of the institutional racism apparent within it.

HATE CRIME

The issue of race also came to be fused with examinations of victimization early on in the move to understand what is termed 'hate crime'. While hate crime is a difficult concept to define, it is largely said to occur when a victim of crime is deliberately targeted by a perpetrator who holds a bias motive due to the victim's real or perceived membership in a certain social group (usually racial groups), but also because of the victim's membership of a religious group, or minority status in regard to sexual orientation, disability, ethnicity, or gender identity. Much of the early literature on hate crime concerned the targeted violence directed at individuals because of their race, but recently hate crime scholarship has examined a range of people who may be disproportionately victimized due to some facet of vulnerability and social marginalization in regard to the vulnerability of their status and identity. Hate crime scholars have studied, for example:

- travelling communities, including Roma and Irish Travellers, migrants, refugees and asylum seekers
- transgender people and the lesbian and gay community
- people with physical and mental disability (and their careers and extended family members)
- members of alternative subcultures (for example, members of extreme music subcultures, e.g. Goths)
- those people who are socially marginalized, such as the street homeless.

However, geographically and internationally there remain differences in countries' perspectives concerning hate crime. In some jurisdictions hate crime is regarded as likely to be associated with perpetrators who belong to right-wing extremist organizations, whereas others tend to suggest that the perpetrators of hate crime are not so exceptional. In England and Wales, where in 2009 there were some 52,102 recorded hate crimes, it is commonly suggested that perpetrators are not largely committed extremists, and the high number of recorded crimes might seem to suggest hate crime is a real problem when compared with European countries that record much lower rates. However, an alternate view is that it reflects a willingness by the authorities to tackle the problem. Indeed, in England and Wales the police record hate crime in accordance with the definition that a hate crime is '[a]ny incident, which may or may not constitute a criminal offence, which is perceived by the victim or any other person, as being motivated by prejudice or hate'. It also perhaps reflects the scrutiny law enforcement agencies have faced after notorious cases such as the suicide of Fiona Pilkington and her daughter Francesca Hardwick; the murder of Zahid Mubarek in Feltham Young Offenders' Institution and the racist murder of Stephen Lawrence.

Further resources

Since the attack on the World Trade Centre in September 2001, and the Bali, London and Madrid bombings, the threat of Islamist terror has become a central concern that also connects with issues of crime and crime control. At the same time some criminologists such as Basia Spalek (2007) have suggested that now rather than simply falling back on the narrow categories of the past such as race, criminology should come to talk of identity. For Spalek, rather than using narrow singular categories of analysis, criminologists must understand broader identity politics, and the multiplicity of facets of human identity, such as gender, race, class, age, religion and sexuality, which are often interwoven and interconnected and which contribute to the experiences of both crime and victimization. You might want to read Spalek and Rowe's texts and think about how race has been replaced by discourse on religion in the context of contemporary criminal justice debates.

Students looking for an excellent text can do no better than Mike Rowe's excellent and comprehensive *Race and Crime* (2012). While it is now quite dated, *Race, Crime and Criminal Justice* by Bowling and Phillips (2002) is still an accessible and readable text. Bowling's *Violent Racism* (1999) is still perhaps the classic study of racially motivated hate crime in the United Kingdom but the subject has moved on significantly in recent years, and therefore a more contemporary text dealing with the topic of hate crime is Neil Chakraborti and Jon Garland's (2009) *Hate Crime: Impacts, Causes, Responses*, which is an indispensable guide to more recent debates and developments in this field.

2.11 PENOLOGY

Core Areas

What is penology?

Why punish?

A brief history of British prisons

Historical phases of punishment

Prisons today and the future of prisons

RUNNING THEMES

Imprisonment and its effects and use should never be removed from **ideological** considerations, and therefore the stance that people take on imprisonment will be influenced by their opinions and their beliefs in the purpose of punishment. Of course, there will also always be **political** and **economic** considerations that will inform how imprisonment is used. Clearly, imprisonment and removing an individual's liberty is about the exercise of **power** by the state. Imprisonment should be considered in light of what we know about **gender**, **class** and **race** as there is a common theme of **inequality** when these factors are linked to imprisonment.

KEY THINKER

Michel Foucault (1926–84) was a French sociologist interested in the relationship between power and knowledge (a theme that is evident in the majority of his work). The power/knowledge complex is based on the idea that power and knowledge are intimately connected, and each is reliant upon the other. With regard to the prison, Foucault suggests that power is not intrinsic in the institution, but in the techniques of discipline on which the prison draws. Foucault traces the development of institutions that draw upon discipline – such as the system of prisons, suggesting that there has been a visible spread in social control – and the growth of disciplinary society as a whole. *Discipline and Punish* (1977) documented the shift from corporal to carceral punishment between the late eighteenth and mid-nineteenth century.

WHAT IS PENOLOGY?

Traditionally the term 'penology' has been used to detail the academic study of penal institutions (in the most part, prisons). Penology, like criminology, has drawn from a diverse range of academic traditions; from psychology, medicine and economics through to social sciences. Traditionally, the term penology was in the most part associated with attempts to reform and rationalize penal conditions (such as in the work of John Howard and Jeremy Bentham), but more recently, penology's focus broadened. Penology can now be seen to include the systematic inquiry into the characteristics of the penal institution (for example, the work of Goffman, 1961) and inquiry into the effectiveness of custody (this includes some work on the subject of legal theories and theories of punishment).

WHY PUNISH?

Theories about the purpose of punishment will necessarily underpin a large amount of penology. Those academics who write about and study imprisonment often have different and conflicting views about what prison should be for – what an individual regards as the purpose of imprisonment will clearly have an impact upon whether they regard punishment as effective or not. There are a number of competing views of the purposes of punishment, and you should be aware of these. Practically, prison is used to hold people on remand (those who are awaiting trial but have been refused bail for fear that they will flee, interfere with the process of the law or commit further crimes), as a threat to support non-custodial sentences and as a punishment in its own right. Beyond the practical purposes there are a number of ideological justifications for imprisonment that have been used by a range of academics to support their arguments about imprisonment.

The symbolic function (denunciation) – By removing offenders from society and placing restrictions upon their liberty and freedoms, prison fulfils a symbolic function – it sends out a powerful message to both offenders and non-offenders that criminal behaviour is not tolerated and will evoke sanction. Prisons express the collective disapproval of the public for the actions of the offender. Often, Victorian local prisons are large buildings toward the centre of cities. Their architecture and positioning are perhaps good reminders of how the symbolic function of prison was actively conveyed to citizens.

Incapacitation – This is the idea that punishment generally (and prison specifically) actively serve to prevent people committing more crime. The offender's liberty is curtailed so that the individual is rendered physically incapable of further offending. Clearly, while someone is in prison it is difficult for them to commit offences against the community at large for the length of their incarceration, but the notion of incapacitation informs a range of punishments. For example, in the 1960s, attendance centres were developed to prevent football hooligans from attending matches, and driving bans and electronic tagging can also serve as a means of incapacitating offenders.

Deterrence – This describes the notion that the threat of some form of consequence can serve to dissuade people from a course of action, and encourage them to abide by society's rules. The principle of deterrence was the basis of Beccaria's classical criminological work (1764), but has also been influential with politicians and academics, often (though not exclusively) those on the political right.

Rehabilitation – The concept of rehabilitation is often linked with treatment, and describes a concern with reforming or rehabilitating offenders, whether by personal example, or through training, education, work experience, or exposing offenders to treatment programmes, group work, and counselling. Such an approach views the sentence of imprisonment and the associated loss of liberty as the punishment, and argues for positive prison regimes that are humane and progressive in the belief that they can reduce the future occurrence of crime.

Retributivism – Essentially, the term 'retributive' suggests that the reason for punishing offenders is because they deserve it. The future consequences of the punishment are not an issue that needs to be considered; quite simply when the offender committed the offence they 'earned' the punishment.

Abolitionism – This is another important strand of thought on imprisonment that influences penology. Abolitionism isn't really a theory about the purpose of punishment but about its delivery. If prison damages people and does them more harm than good (because of factors such as its negative effects upon employment prospects, its tendency to institutionalize, brutalize and sever family ties), should we use it at all? Abolitionists argue that because of the damage done by prison, we should remove or restrict its use. In the most extreme form, abolitionists call for the wholesale removal of prison sanctions, but most current abolitionists argue for prison to be a last resort and only used when necessary with the most serious and dangerous offenders.

A BRIEF HISTORY OF BRITISH PRISONS

There is not really time to detail the whole history of the development of the British prison system, but many of criminology's core works are related to the development of punishment and forms of social control (see Foucault, 1977, and Garland, 2002). It is worthwhile to have a knowledge not only of the theory with which we explain punishment and imprisonment, but also of some of the most important historical events in terms of British prisons and the prison timeline shown below should help you somewhat toward that end.

Prison timeline

1777 – John Howard, religious reformer and former High Sheriff of Bedfordshire publishes *The State of the Prison in England and Wales* and describes the system of local prisons as 'filthy, corrupt ridden and unhealthy'.

1779 – 'Hard labour' is introduced by parliament and prisoners are held on prison hulks (old ships) anchored in the river Thames. The use of these hulks is only discontinued in 1857.

1810 – The Holford Committee is established by parliament as a forum to debate imprisonment. They make the decision to build the first state penitentiary (Millbank) that will reform offenders through solitary confinement and rigorous religious instruction.

1816 – The first state-built prison, Millbank, opens in Central London.

1823 – Under Home Secretary Robert Peel, the Goal Act is passed. This attempted to separate prisoners according to the crimes they had committed, but proved largely ineffectual in practice.

1835 – The Prisons Act makes provisions for the appointment of five inspectors of prisons, while the dominant ideology remains isolating prisoners so that they cannot be a bad influence upon one another, a continuation of the ideas which informed the Goal Act in 1823.

1862–68 – Both public flogging (in 1862) and transportation (in 1868) are abolished as punishments.

1887 – The Prison Act 1887 first brought prisons under the control of the Home Secretary in Britain. Prior to this, prisons were administered locally by Justices of the Peace. Administration of the prison system is made the responsibility of a prison commission, and the first head of the commission Sir Edmund Du Cane is appointed. He is unflinching in his belief that prison should punish, and installs a harsh regime for prisoners.

1895 – The Gladstone Committee is progressive and suggests that a core function of prison should be to 'reform'. The recommendations are embraced by new head of the prison commission Sir Evelyn Ruggles Bryce. Prison conditions and regimes begin to improve.

1895–1960s – This was an era of progressive penal policy and practice in Britain.

1960s – The first crisis of security and the Mountbatten report – a number of high profile escapes, including those by the Great Train Robbers and the spy George Blake leads to an increased focus upon security – with resources increasingly targeted at preventing escape.

(Continued)

(Continued)

1974 – Robert Martinson publishes his 'What Works?' article, which questions the effectiveness of treatment. With the political right gaining influence there is a decline in the influence of 'treatment' and welfare approaches and an increased belief that prison is effective as a means of incapacitation.

1990 – The Strangeways Riot – the largest prison disturbance in Britain – sparks a wave of riots and protests in other institutions, and highlights how stark and bleak conditions have become in prison, where an emphasis on security and overcrowded local prisons is brought to light.

1991 – Lord Woolfe's report into the Strangeways riot is published. It is extremely critical of the management and regime in prisons, and the lack of humanity and justice shown to prisoners, especially those on remand. The Criminal Justice Act makes provision for the contracting out of court escort services.

1992 – The Criminal Justice Act is extended to allow for new private prisons to be built to hold convicted prisoners.

1993 – Michael Howard makes his now famous 'Prison works' speech to the Conservative party conference, which is inspired by American right realist Charles Murray. This is also the year that two-year-old James Bulger is murdered by two ten-year-old boys; an event that many criminologists regard as a catalyst for steep increases in the use of prison. Similarly, legislation allows for all state prisons to be privately managed, with a target that 10 per cent of prisons should be managed in this way.

1994 – The Woodcock Report into the escape of armed prisoners from the special security unit at Whitemoor prison is extremely critical of lax security at the prison.

1995 – Three life sentence prisoners escape from Parkhurst Prison. The Learmont Report is once again highly critical of security; Michael Howard sacks the Director General of the Prison Service, Derek Lewis. The legacy of the Parkhurst and Whitemoor escapes is increased security.

1997 – New Labour is elected to power having promised to reverse prison privatization. However, once elected they continue its use.

1998 – Wormwood Scrubs prison is subjected to a police investigation that eventually sees three officers jailed for violence against prisoners and six officers dismissed (including three who had been convicted and cleared on appeal). Eventually the Prison Service admits that its officers subjected some inmates to sustained beatings, mock executions, death threats, choking and torrents of racist abuse.

2000 – Zahid Mubarek is attacked by his racist cellmate in his cell at Feltham Young Offenders' Institution. He died seven days later. The government's repeated attempts to block a public inquiry led to a four-and-a-half year delay between the murder and the inquiry.

2003 – A review under the leadership of businessman Patrick Carter recommends the merger of the prison and probation service into the National Offender Management Service (NOMS). The government accepts this recommendation and work begins toward a merger.

2005 – The prison population in England and Wales reaches 76,226 on the first of July, its highest ever. It is predicted to rise to above 80,000 shortly, and be 90,000 by the end of the decade.

2007 – After a period characterized by changes of political leadership, crises about foreign national prisoners, and a burgeoning prison population, on 9 May 2007 the correctional services element of the Home Office is moved to join the former Department of Constitutional Affairs in the newly created Ministry of Justice. The Labour government also first announces plans for three 'Titan' prisons which will hold up to 2,500 prisoners each.

2008 – In January, the Secretary of State for Justice announces a major organizational reform which results in the Director-General of Her Majesty's Prison Service, Phil Wheatley, becoming the Chief Executive of NOMS, and assuming responsibility for both the National Probation Service (NPS) as well as HM Prison Service and management of contracts for private sector operation of prisons and prisoner escorting.

2009 – The government's plans for Titan prisons are dropped.

2010 – In the run up to the May parliamentary election, the Conservatives announce that they are considering the use of prison ships as part of their plans for criminal justice. On the election of a coalition Conservative and Liberal Democrat government, the coalition states it believed that we need radical action to reform our criminal justice system. The central strand of future policy is to be greater investment in rehabilitation as a means of making fiscal savings, although there is little direct mention of prison policy. In December 2010 the Green Paper 'Breaking the Cycle' introduces 'payment by results' for offender rehabilitation schemes alongside substantial reforms to sentencing which will reduce the use of custody. The introduction of the paper states: 'We will ensure that criminals make amends for their crimes and better repair the harm they have caused to victims and society as a whole.'

2011 – In the wake of the August 2011 riots, toward the end of 2011, the UK prison population hits an all-time high of 88,179.

HISTORICAL PHASES OF PUNISHMENT

Prison and punishment are evolutionary, and many academics have documented change in the administration of punishment. Michel Foucault's (1977) suggestion that the development of prison can be linked to the emergence of a disciplinary industrial society has been built upon by academics, such as David Garland (2001a), who broadly divide punishment into three phases.

Phase 1

The first phase was marked by the use of capital and corporal punishment, prior to the increasing reliance upon prison. This is a time when capital punishment was commonplace largely prior to the birth of industrial society. Humanitarians and religious reformers such as those of the 'classical school' challenge the harsh and erratic nature of punishment.

Phase 2

The second phase witnesses society's industrialization, and with it the spread of a discipline society. Capital and corporal punishments are reduced and instead 'carceral' punishment takes its place: prison, reformatories and poor houses. The ideology that underpins such notions is more welfare-orientated and new disciplines such as psychiatry and psychology offer the potential solutions for treating and reforming offenders, and instilling discipline spreads.

Phase 3

The third phase occurs post-1960s and is set against a backdrop of increased political discussion about crime and punishment. This phase also witnesses the decline in welfarism, the belief that 'nothing works' and a growing public 'punitivism'. Notions of treatment decline, to be replaced by the concept of 'risk management'. Levels of incarceration rise and we witness the birth of mass incarceration. The spread of technology means that custody extends beyond the prison wall and into society more generally (for example, satellite monitoring, or electronic tagging).

PRISONS TODAY AND THE FUTURE OF PRISONS

In both America and Britain from the late 1970s there has been a largely unbroken trend of increased prison numbers. This has accompanied what I have termed the move toward Phase 3 in imprisonment, the shift from rehabilitative to post-welfare mass imprisonment (Parenti, 1999; Garland, 2001b). As the crisis in prison numbers grows ever greater in the capitalist west, it is likely that prisons and imprisonment, their legitimacy and the existence of a 'crisis', will be the subject of fierce academic debate for years to come. Indeed, recently the move for abolitionism has resurfaced. For example, Scott and Codd's *Controversial Issues in Prison* (2010) is a passionate plea to 'regard the idea of a 'healthy prison' being 'an contradictory to the present reality of most imprisonment. They argue that prisons are places of 'sadness and terror, harm and injustice, secrecy and oppression'. Scrutinizing a range of controversial issues such as mental health problems in prison, women in prison, children and young people in custody, race and racism, and self-inflicted deaths they argue that such issues raise fundamental concerns 'about the legitimacy of the confinement project and the kind of society in which it is deemed essential' (p.ix). As such, their suggestion is a return to the politics of nothing less than the abolition of prison so that it eventually becomes 'but a distant memory', arguing that nobody is truly safe in such a toxic environment and that 'the penal apparatus of the Capitalist State has blood on its hands' (2010: 169–170). Similarly, eminent sociologist Loïc Wacquant has argued that the prison is an 'outlaw institution' and suggests that the carceral boom in the United States results from the penalization of poverty caused by erosion of the of the economic, welfare and justice missions of the state. Wacquant suggests that pro-market think tanks have played a driving role in fashioning and diffusing America's 'punitive common sense' across the Atlantic, thus accelerating the import of aggressive crime control policies in Western Europe by political elites (including left-leaning governments) seduced by free market and anti-welfare ideology. Wacquant argues that while the prison purports to enforce the law and to curtail the disorders generated by economic deregulation policies, the very organization and daily operation of prisons make them outlaw institutions which while promoted as a remedy for insecurity and social marginality, actually serves to concentrate and intensify both (Wacquant, 2012). To what extent such arguments will serve to decrease the use of imprisonment remains to be seen, and certainly there has been talk of a move away from using prison as part of a more general austerity drive in both England and Wales and in some parts of the USA. However, despite that, since the recent riots and under the new Conservative/Liberal coalition government in the UK, prison numbers have again reached an all-time high. All that seems certain is that the function and use of imprisonment will remain a key part of criminological debate in coming years.

Further resources

Robert Martinson is an academic remembered for his study of the lack of effectiveness of rehabilita-tive schemes which began in the era of prison expansionism in the 1970s in the USA. Read Martinson's (1974) work in order to critically evaluate the proposition that any decline in rehabilitative approaches is driven by political motivation and the growing politics of law and order. Perhaps you might try read-ing Martinson's arguments and see whether you agree with how they have been represented.

Michael Cavadino and James Dignan's (2007) *The Penal System* is now in its fourth edition and is an extremely comprehensive and authoritative account of the issues surrounding imprisonment. Jewkes' (2007) *Handbook on Prisons* is a very comprehensive and useful text.

2.12   SERIOUS CRIME

CORE AREAS

White collar crime

Organizational and corporate crimes

Professional crime

Organized crime

Transnational crime

Terrorism

War crimes and genocide

The crimes of everyday to crimes of the state

RUNNING THEMES

I have used the term 'serious crime' to describe a range of criminal activity. For criminologists examining white collar crimes, issues of **power** and **representa-tion** are combined. They suggest (in the critical/conflict tradition) that the crimes of the powerful are given very little attention and that most criminol-ogy is driven by the perception that the crimes committed by the relatively powerless are prioritized. This form of criminology seeks to challenge and reconsider what constitutes criminal acts, arguing that a wider appreciation of criminal activity is necessary; and criminologists should broaden their focus to examine crimes of the state and crimes of the elite.

KEY THINKER

Edwin H. Sutherland (1883–1950). The concept of white collar crime (WCC) stems from the work of American Sociologist Edwin H. Sutherland who specifically sought an opportunity to prove that his theory of differential association (see Chapter 2.3) could account for all forms of criminality. Sutherland defined WCC as '[a] crime committed by a person of responsibility in the course of his [*sic*] occupation' (Sutherland, 1945; 1949) a definition that has now been heavily criticized (see below). However, it should be noted that by shifting the attention away from the emphasis on poverty and other problems located amongst the lower socioeconomic classes (that was so dominant in the criminology of the time), Sutherland had set the scene for conflict theories and promoted the idea that crime was something that spanned all classes.

What images does the word crime evoke in your mind? Most of us, if we were to be honest, would immediately think about crime being serious, and would probably think of crimes such as murder, robbery, theft and burglary. We associate crime with inner-city areas, with poverty and harshness of life. It is not surprising therefore that when criminologists examine crime, when politicians and the public discuss it and the media report it, it is just these sorts of 'crimes of the street' that are represented. Few of us associate crime with wealthy businessmen in expensive suits, yet nevertheless, that is perhaps where crime is at its most prevalent and has the greatest cost to society. This chapter examines serious crime, which is largely crime involving more powerful and privileged actors.

WHITE COLLAR CRIME

Sutherland argued that crimes are committed by the rich and powerful, including 'white collar workers' (who are a higher occupational class than their blue collar counterparts). White collar offenders were executive and business manager level. Sutherland argued that those of a higher status, and enjoying a higher degree of trust, were also frequently likely to be the perpetrators of a range of crimes and misdemeanours, but were less likely to be detected and prosecuted. As you will already be aware, Sutherland was keen for criminology to extend its focus beyond the notion of crime, and to examine socially harmful activity (see Chapter 1.5).

> White collar crime is regarded by most criminologists as potentially far more harmful and serious than other types of crime. However, it is infrequently acknowledged in such a way by society generally, and may tend to be little conceived or understood by many members of society.

'White collar crime' as a category has been used to refer to an extremely diverse and varied collection of criminal activities, from smaller frauds committed by junior office staff in small businesses, to multi-million pound frauds committed by the directors of multinational corporations. Therefore what constitutes white collar crime is not really agreed upon. Instead the term tends to be deployed in a varying fashion. However, in the most part the term still describes:

- offences committed by people of high/or relatively high status
- offences committed in the workplace by people who enjoy fairly privileged positions of trust
- offences that are made possible by legitimate employment
- typical offences considered under this category, including: accounting malpractice, frauds, embezzlement, tax evasion/violation and workplace related thefts.

There are immediate problems with the concept of white collar crime: What do we mean by high status? How should we define and measure it? How do we measure and categorize privilege? Although Sutherland makes it quite clear that he is detailing the higher echelons of organizational hierarchy, the term 'white collar crime' has often been used to categorize any crime that is not committed by manual (or blue collar) workers. The problem with this approach is that it tends to move away from the original concern with examining the illegitimate behaviour of the privileged. As the problems with identifying exactly what constitutes 'white collar crime' are many, some academics, such as Richard Quinney (1980[1977]) have argued that the term 'white collar crime' should be replaced, and all crimes committed in the course of employment should be referenced under the heading 'occupational crime'.

Hazel Croall suggests that 'the enormous range of activities encompassed by the category of white collar crime has inevitably led to attempts to divide it into sub-categories, to provide researchers with a manageable group of offences and enable comparisons between offences' (Croall, 2001: 11). It is therefore important that criminologists do not consider 'white collar crime' as a set of neat, easily-defined offences.

The most significant debate around white collar crime in recent years has been that involving the distinction between *occupational* and *organizational* crime.

- Occupational crime is the category given by Quinney where people commit crime in the course of their employment, in the main for personal gain.
- Organizational crime is essentially corporate crime, where the aim is to further the purposes of the company, but not necessarily the individual.

What are not disputed by most criminologists are the serious potential implications of failures in individual and corporate practices. Carlson's (1981) study of the loss of life in the exploration for oil in the North Sea (confirmed by later events such as the explosions and fire on the Piper Alpha oil rig in 1988, with the loss of 168 lives), for instance, showed that many lives could have been saved with rudimentary attention to safety considerations. The chemical explosion at the Union Carbide Company in Bhopal in 1984 (which killed 2,600 people) serves as an example of how great the cost can be when companies breach health and safety regulations. Yet such crimes are often committed in areas where poverty is already endemic, as in the case of Bhopal, or more recently in 2006, in the case of the dumping of toxic waste in Ivory Coast by oil trading company Trafigura.

There are, however, some criminologists who have contested the idea that white collar crime should constitute an area of study for criminologists. For Gottfredson and Hirschi (1990), much white collar crime mirrors traditional crime, and can be explained using 'control theory' (offenders seek immediate gratification) which renders the setting of the crime and the status of the offender an irrelevance. Other criminologists have been quick to ridicule the notion of white collar crime; hence prominent right realist James Q. Wilson's dismissive suggestion that: 'People do not bar and nail shut their windows, avoid going out at night or harbor deep suspicions about strangers because of unsafe working conditions or massive consumer fraud' (1975).

ORGANIZATIONAL AND CORPORATE CRIMES

Sutherland's work proved influential in that it led criminologists to question the occurrence of crime as part of capitalism, influencing conflict criminology, much of which was Marxist inspired and critical of capitalism and its institutions. This in turn influenced criminologists to turn their attention to how crime and business could be linked and resulted in the study of organizational or corporate crime.

> The term 'corporate crime' is used to refer to both acts and omissions that are the result of deliberate decisions or negligence in legitimate businesses. These acts are undertaken not to benefit an individual or individuals, but by individuals in order to benefit the corporation itself, and therefore reflect upon the culture of the company. By breaking laws (both civil and criminal) it is possible for companies, for example, to chase greater profits at the cost of employee or public safety. Such an activity is not individually motivated but part of the ethos of the company. While it may sometimes be called 'organizational' crime it should not be confused with 'organized' crime.

PROFESSIONAL CRIME

Once again the term 'professional crime' can trace its origins to Edwin Sutherland and specifically his life history study of Chic Conwell (who actually wrote the majority of the text), *The Professional Thief* (1937). Sutherland suggests that being a professional thief required that one made a living by exclusively committing thefts, and using all of one's working hours illegitimately. The core intention of this work was to provide empirical support for the concepts that criminal activity is planned, and more importantly learned by 'differential association'.

The notion of criminal careers continued to gain influence in criminology however, the term 'criminal career' has bypassed and replaced the notion of 'professional crime'. The problem with this is that they do not necessarily refer to the same thing. Those involved in crime will all have a criminal career, even if it is short; the notion of professional criminality conveys a sense of the persistent commitment that some, but by no means all offenders have to crime. However, professional crime is inherently difficult to define, as you have to ask on what grounds do we assess 'professionalism' in terms of crime, by competence or commitment? Who constitutes the professional criminal? However, the term has been used by criminologists examining some more serious and organized forms of criminality.

ORGANIZED CRIME

It is perhaps unsurprising that most of the discussion of organized crime emanates from America around the 1920s, an era where prohibition of alcohol created the climate for 'bootleggers' to accumulate vast personal wealth through the illegal sale of alcohol. However, over time it has emerged as a concept to be used by both academics and political groups; emerging again as an area of interest in the post-communist era, until 2001 when both political groups and academics turned their attention to new criminal threats to national security from organized criminal gangs such as the Russian mafia. In recent years, and post-September 11, this concern is being replaced with the threat of terrorism, somewhat displacing discussions about organized crime.

Indeed in the wake of the terrorist attacks on the London underground on 7 July 2005, the need to tackle organized crime has really been eclipsed by discussions about terrorism. Perhaps what is notable here is that, very often, the two can coexist, and it has long been known that terrorist organizations often have links to highly organized forms of criminality. In the aftermath of the terrorist attacks in London, debate quickly turned to the failure of legislation allowing criminals to be tracked across national borders. However, there has been less attention paid to the way the political actions of some state governments have served to assist such groups previously, although there has been some discussion about how some state governments actively continue to support and cultivate terrorism.

The specific threat of organized crime is apparent in that criminal behaviour associated with professional crime threatens and relies upon institutions of power, for example, corrupting government figures, 'buying people off', and bid rigging. Similarly, many of the activities of large criminal groups mirror the activities of the state, exacting money, threatening the state's core functions of protection, extraction and coercion along with the state's monopoly on force (Naylor, 1997).

TRANSNATIONAL CRIME

The concept of transnational crime relies a great deal on the sociological concept of globalization, which is a term that sociologists use to describe the way the world is transformed into a single global system; and the way in which the world is shrinking with the introduction of new technology, the expansion of international trade and the international distribution of labour.

Globalization and the changing nature of the world create new criminal opportunities – some via new technology such as computers and the internet, some because of the expansion of markets. Globalization is an important element, as whilst transnational crime has occurred for many years (think of smuggling as an example, which has occurred for centuries) the changing world we live in clearly presents new opportunities for criminals. What is meant by transnational crime, is crime that involves a fairly high degree of sophistication and organization, often the endeavour of criminal gangs who can use national borders to avoid law enforcement agencies.

Some key features of transnational crime

- At the most basic level, transnational crime is crime that crosses national boundaries, and therefore crosses different countries with different laws and law enforcement agencies.
- It is regarded in the most part as sophisticated – the product of calculating criminal gangs.
- It often involves illicit markets, such as the traffic in illegal drugs, firearms, products made from endangered species, people trafficking.
- Some items, however, may be legal, such as smuggling of legal goods to avoid paying duty (such as tobacco, alcohol or antiques).
- It may well involve corruption and using legitimate companies as a front: corruption underlies a great deal of transnational crime (bribing officials, moving and laundering money).
- Statutory controls such as immigration controls or high taxes create the markets that transnational criminals rely upon.
- Moral campaigners have highlighted the trade in human organs and children and babies sold for adoption, but again these issues are less frequently considered as transnational crime.

TERRORISM

Much like crime, in the international community, terrorism has no universally agreed, legally binding definition. While common attempts at defining terrorism generally refer to those violent acts which are intended to create fear (terror), are perpetrated for a religious, political or, ideological goal, and those which deliberately target or disregard the safety of non-combatants or civilians, the concept is fluid and complex. However, in the era post 9/11 with 'the war on terror', issues such as security, terrorism, and 'radicalization' have all increasingly become part of the lexicon of criminology, due to its relationships with legal processes and law enforcement. Indeed, in recent years there has been a highlighting of the use of similar tactics by criminality and terrorism, and the links between the two.

The word 'terrorism' is politically and emotionally charged, and this greatly compounds the difficulty of providing a precise definition. The concept often proves controversial as it is used by state authorities (and individuals with access to state support) to delegitimize political or other opponents and potentially legitimize the state's own use of armed force against opponents (such use of force may itself be described as 'terror' by opponents of the state), such as when authoritarian regimes describe political opponents as terrorists, as happened widely during the Arab spring. Moreover, there will be discussions about whether actions of violent, politically motivated individuals such as Anders Behring Breivik, who killed 77 people in a bomb attack and gun spree in Norway, ought to be considered terrorists, or merely criminals, just as there has been with Islamic extremists in the UK in recent years. Of course, offending for political reasons may also challenge some of the traditional theories and explanations offered by theoretical criminology, again making the concept of terrorism relevant to criminology, and vice versa making criminology useful to the understanding of terrorism.

WAR CRIMES AND GENOCIDE

War crimes are acts that are criminal and remain criminal, even though they are committed by individuals or groups at a time of war or armed conflict when acting under military orders. Acts such as murder, torture, ill treatment or slave labour of civilians, the murder or torture of prisoners of war, the killing of hostages, and the destroying of property or civilian settlements unnecessarily, could all constitute war crimes. Members of armed forces, militias, or civilians who violate such laws can be tried by international and national courts and military tribunals. It is not a defence to cite acting under orders, however, superior officers hold a responsibility for those under their direction unless they have evidently attempted to suppress them. The 1949 Geneva Convention clarified the war crimes accepted by the Nuremburg Trial of leading Nazis, and subsequent rules have extended the protections available to soldiers and civilians at times of conflict. However, this has not prevented such crimes, which not only include the massacre of civilians in Srebrenica and Rwanda, but also those which are occuring in the now occupied Iraq, and are the preserve of both British and American soldiers. Some criminologists have highlighted the failure of criminology to adequately examine war crime.

Genocide refers to organized acts of crime that are committed during either conflict or peace, and intend to exterminate all or part of a national, religious, racial or ethnic group. It differs from what is termed 'ethnic cleansing' because it is state-sponsored and organized, as in the case of the treatment of the Jews by the Nazi regime in Germany. Genocide is regarded by the United Nations General Assembly to be the most serious crime against humanity, however, once again, criminologists have been slow to regard this as a viable field of inquiry. Genocide, like war crime and all of the crimes above, is largely committed by those who are privileged, yet any searching of criminology textbooks will quickly reveal the fact that it is a crime that criminologists have ignored. This perhaps serves as further evidence of criminologist's failure to engage with the crimes of the powerful and elite due to their preoccupation with crimes of the street.

"Has criminology as a subject adequately recognized or addressed the crimes of the powerful?"

This question or similar questions about the focus of criminology are often seen as a gift by students in exams because they allow you to expand a debate to a wide range of areas. However, you should beware of the 'all I know about' answer because, all too frequently, students rush into writing something that ends up very jumbled and mixed. Try to write to a structure; so you might want to say, 'there are a variety of areas that I could examine [give examples] but in this instance I will focus upon the crimes of the state specifically'. If you do this, then make sure that you stay to the brief you set yourself. Remember to draw upon theory (in this case the work of conflict and left idealist criminologists lends empirical support). Remember to use and cite theorists, so you can mention specific contributions made by academics. If doing this in exams try to remember the date and title of publications, as it shows you have done some revision.

THE CRIMES OF EVERYDAY TO CRIMES OF THE STATE

There have been continual debates about just what sort of crime criminologists should be concerned with, and many criminologists recognize that for the most part the subject is concerned with the crimes of the street, those visible offences that tend to define the parameters of what for most people would constitute crime – minor thefts, vandalism, minor assaults and the like. Indeed, the vast volume crime of everyday life, or everyday crime is just that. In the UK in recent years there has arguably been an expansion of control through legislation so that 'anti-social behaviour' rather than crime is now subject to increased regulatory control. However, while arguably we should take these everyday harms for what they are – which is damaging and harmful to communities – the harms that these crimes inflict are relatively minor, if still existing on a similar continuum of motivation to the most serious offences. For this reason some criminologists such as Penny Green and Tony Ward (2004) have made powerful arguments that the most serious crimes are acts that are largely committed, instigated or condoned by the most powerful and privileged actors, governments and their officials. For example, genocide, war crimes, torture and corruption are often under-acknowledged by academic authors, yet are significantly more socially damaging and harmful than the crimes of the street. Calling such harmful state activities 'crimes' should be uncontroversial as they violate international and/or national criminal law; however, often these activities are hidden. Much like those committed to zemiology, green criminologists, critical criminologists and others who propose a new direction for criminology and recognition of the wider processes of harm, conceive of crime in a broader sense. Indeed, when we think of crime we tend not to think of politicians and the powerful, yet those dwarf the harms of the street. Yet Steve Hall has recently argued, effective criminological theory should not marginalize one or the other category, or set street crimes and state crimes as in binary opposition, but instead seek to explain both. As Hall has argued, the litmus test of theory and the project of criminology may be the discipline's capability to explain all crime from the serious to the minor and answer the question of 'why [some] individuals or corporate bodies are willing to risk the infliction of harm on others in order to further their own instrumental or expressive interests' (Hall, 2012: 1).

Further resources

Is James Q. Wilson right to argue that '[p]eople do not bar and nail shut their windows, avoid going out at night or harbor deep suspicions about strangers because of unsafe working conditions or massive consumer fraud'? Are the crimes of the powerful really threatening or are they an essential part of life?

(Continued)

(Continued)

One of the problems with the crimes of the powerful is that we simply have very little knowledge about the real extent (because of their hidden nature; a point Wilson fails to make). If you had to go about researching corporate or white collar crime, how would begin? What are the difficulties in finding out about victims? Would it ever be possible to overcome these?

Crime: Local and Global (Muncie et al., 2009) is a useful text that covers a range of issues related to serious crime. John Minkes and Leonard Minkes' (2008) edited collection *Corporate and White Collar Crime* is a useful text.

2.13   CYBERCRIME

C<small>ORE</small> A<small>REAS</small>

Introducing cybercrime

What is cybercrime – something new or old crime gone global?

Measuring cyber offending – the scope and scale

Cybercriminals – what do they look like?

RUNNING THEMES

'Cybercrime' is a term that is used to describe a range of criminal activity. As we previously considered, historically most criminology is driven by a perception that crimes are committed by the relatively powerless, but committed in a public, physical space. However, transformations in technology have forced criminology to reconsider the space, place and character of what constitutes criminal acts, arguing that a wider appreciation of criminal activity and a broader focus is necessary, to examine new spaces where crime occurs, such as the internet.

KEY THINKER

David S. Wall is a Professor of Criminology who researches the subjects of crime and technology, criminology, criminal justice, and policing, and has written extensively on cybercrime and issues such as intellectual property crime (coun-terfeiting). His most notable publication on the topic of cybercrime is *Cybercrime: The Transformation of Crime in the Information Age* (2007) which sets out differ-ent typologies of cybercrime and the transformative test (see below). Wall also argues that the increase in personal computing power available within a glo-balized communications network has affected both the nature of, and responses to criminal activities. Drawing on empirical research findings and multidisci-plinary sources, he goes on to argue that we are beginning to experience a new generation of automated cybercrimes, which are almost completely mediated by networked technologies that are themselves converging.

INTRODUCING CYBERCRIME

Traditionally criminology has been concerned with crime that occurs between people involved in face to face, real time interaction. Crime tends to bring vic-tim and offender together in a physical space and a social setting. However, in recent years technological advances have impacted massively on how we live our lives and how we interact with people. New technologies such as mobile phones and computers have allowed people to communicate across space in a way that perhaps would have been unthinkable just a few years ago.

Computers, the internet and electronic communications play an ever-increas-ing part in our lives, with the use of the internet now standard and continuing to grow. Mobile internet devices, such as smart phones, are now common, as is access to the online world or the cyber environment, which allows people to communicate and interact across geographical boundaries and borders. The internet has changed all manner of facets of everyday life: how we speak and communicate with one another; how we conduct business; how we shop, social-ize and spend our recreational and leisure time and seek out pleasure. People engage with cyber environments in different ways, and these new settings raise immediate questions that are relevant to social scientists. Are new online envi-ronments utopian spaces of freedom and anonymity or are they regulated spaces subject to monitoring and surveillance? What harms exist in cyber environ-ments and what threats exist to users? What opportunities do cyber environ-ments present for criminal behaviours and controlling criminal behaviour? What is the relationship between cyberspace and the real world?

Criminologists are now turning their attention to the cyber environment and the internet, although there is still a great deal of debate about how crime operates on the internet. In the first instance this was largely to examine how the cyber world would impact on criminal behaviour, as criminologists asked whether the internet simply facilitated a new ways of committing old, familiar and well established crimes such as fraud. This sentiment is well captured by Grabosky's question of whether it was simply 'old wine, new bottles' (2001) or whether it was an arena for completely new crimes that hadn't existed before to occur and a space for new forms of transgressive behaviour.

Much in keeping with cultural criminology, many of the academics writing about cybercrime draw heavily on the notion of social transgression, the violating of norms. Of course the internet offers new possibilities for transgression. The internet is a revolutionary technology that enables millions of individuals across the globe to access, exchange, and appraise vast amounts of information. It is a vast network system that processes data and information between innumerable sites in the virtual electronic world called 'cyberspace', that create new liberating opportunities, just as it creates new risks, threats and opportunities for transgression and criminality.

WHAT IS CYBERCRIME – SOMETHING NEW OR OLD CRIME GONE GLOBAL?

The emerging consensus seems to be that the internet presents a space for both old and new crime, and is an arena where some new threats and crimes emerge, for example activities such as hacking (gaining unauthorized access to computer systems) designing viruses, worms and Trojan horses (disguised malicious software programs that are used to steal, damage, destroy, disrupt and infect computer systems and their data). In contrast, other forms are continuations of long-established criminal enterprises, for example many internet frauds such as the romance dating fraud, are an evolution of old pre-existing crimes such as direct mail scams.

Internationally, both governmental and non-state actors engage in cybercrimes. In the most serious forms of cybercrime, state actors and agencies are involved in sophisticated and high-level espionage, sometimes referred to as 'cyber warfare' and global cyber attacks, which the international legal system is attempting to hold actors accountable for via the International Criminal Court. More commonly, however, most routine forms of cybercrime may be on a lower, less serious level. For example, the world of auction websites may impact massively on traditional crimes such as shoplifting by allowing thieves to sell items stolen from shops through auction websites to unsuspecting buyers. Yet paradoxically, the ease with which some old and already established crimes can operate more effectively through online environments may highlight old concerns and increase awareness of the prevalence of what was once hidden away, such as in the case of child pornography, a topic of increasing criminological concern over the last decade.

The term 'cybercrime' has now certainly entered into everyday usage, but often the term is not used in a considered way, and is simply used as a catch all for any crime that is related to cyberspace. David S. Wall, who is perhaps the leading criminologist writing on the topic of cybercrime, has argued that rather than applying the term as a catch-all, we should seek to more carefully consider the different forms of cybercrime that exist. He suggests that there are essentially three different forms of cybercrime:

i **Traditional cybercrime** – This category covers the types of cybercrime that would continue to exist without the internet, but have adapted with new technological innovation and now benefit from, or become more prevalent and/or effective because of the internet. For example, child pornography existed before the internet, often in the form of magazines and videos, but would be traded person to person. The internet simply provides a vehicle that makes such trade far easier for paedophiles. Therefore 'traditional' cybercrime covers activities such as trade in child pornography, the distribution of hate materials, stalking, and the sale of illegal medicines or narcotics.

ii **Hybrid cybercrime** – This category falls somewhere between true and traditional cybercrime and blends elements of both. Like traditional cybercrime this category contains behaviours that can exist offline, but unlike that category, offences in this group have not simply benefited from the opportunities provided by cyberspace, but rather older crimes have evolved and changed in nature due to the opportunity the internet grants. So for example, offences that would fall into this category would be large-scale frauds and identity frauds and entrapment scams.

iii **True cybercrime** – This refers to those categories of crime that exist within and are wholly restricted to cyberspace, and covers the type of offences that are of such a nature that were the internet to be removed, the offence simply could not happen any longer. So, for example, while dating scams could still take place through different forms of communication such as telephone lines or mail, the theft of items in the cyber-realm such as video games (such as second life) hacking and spamming, or maliciously using worms to damage and infect people's computers simply could not exist without the internet.

MEASURING CYBER OFFENDING — THE SCOPE AND SCALE

According to the Cabinet Office and information intelligence experts Detica, in 2011 the UK government estimates that the overall cost to the UK economy from cybercrime is £27bn per year. More specifically, the UK's current cybercrime strategy estimates that the cost from credit card fraud where the consumer's card was used without them present was £328m in 2008–9 (an increase of 13 per cent from the previous year), while crimes that involved stealing the innovation and design of music and film in the UK were estimated at £180m in 2008–9, and the annual loss to the economy from unresolved delivery problems with online sales is estimated to be worth as much as £55m per year.

- In 2008, 55,389 phishing website hosts were detected, an increase of 66 per cent over 2007.
- A 192 per cent increase in spam was detected across the internet, from 119.6 billion messages in 2007 to 349.6 billion in 2008. The most common type of spam detected in 2008 was related to internet or computer related goods and services, which made up 24 per cent of all detected spam.
- Identity fraud continues to increase, and in the first 6 months of 2009, there were 43 per cent more victims of impersonations, a 74 per cent increase in successful identity fraud and a 40 per cent rise in facility takeover fraud (where criminals gain access to legitimately obtained accounts of innocent victims). The cost to the UK economy is at least £1.2 billion and accounts for a criminal cash flow of some £10m per day.
- According to the Internet Watch Foundation Annual Report in 2008, there were some 1,536 individual child abuse domains. Of all known child abuse domains, 58 per cent are housed in the United States.
- It has been suggested that as many as 230,000 people in the UK may have been victims of online romance or dating scams.

CYBERCRIMINALS — WHAT DO THEY LOOK LIKE?

On one hand, some academics tend to suggest that those who use the internet to commit crime are a 'new breed of criminals whose ill-gotten toolkit consists of Central Processing Units, modulator demodulators, war diallers, viruses, and warez' (Corriea and Bowling, 1999: 225). Other criminologists believe that computers are now being employed by some career criminals to commit quite old-fashioned and familiar offences, and that the criminological community could no longer seek to understand offences such as fraud, or for that matter criminal identities, without grasping the place and role of the 'third space'.

What is certain is that cyberspace certainly assists some offenders to commit crimes beyond the traditional physical locations and spaces that they were once limited to. That is not to suggest that place is not important in the understanding of cybercrime. For example, many of the frauds that are perpetrated against those in the rich western countries originate from countries which are poorer and where individuals can struggle to find well paid employment and do not have the benefits of social welfare supports. For example, many dating scams and the eponymous 419 scam (so known because it violates article 419 of the Nigerian Criminal Code) originate in African countries. These forms of crime are often an evolution of advanced fee frauds that previously relied upon letters, and long-established confidence tricks.

However, to think of Russian mafia and organized Nigerian criminal gangs as the only perpetrators of cybercrime perhaps risks overlooking how offenders closer to home use the internet, though some have argued that when we do look close to home, we do not tend to find particularly sophisticated offenders. For example, recent cases involving the Serious Organised Crime Agency (SOCA) in the UK have targeted illegal downloaders and peer to peer file sharers who may not fit with our traditional conceptions of organized criminals. Elsewhere, Treadwell (2012) has argued that more traditional professional criminals exploit the internet to sell counterfeit products, but that those committing cybercrime are the 'usual suspects and not necessarily those well versed in the complexities of computer programming'. Indeed, given the dearth of literature and research that is actually undertaken with cybercrime offenders about their backgrounds, methods and techniques it appears difficult to make a strong assertion about what makes cybercriminals different to those traditionally studied by criminologists.

What seems certain is that as more and more of our personal details and private assets are stored or accessible electronically rather than physically, and the more material that is stored in or available in locations outside the national jurisdiction, the more opportunities there will be for crime. However, the same technologies can be used to protect ourselves and by our law enforcement agencies to detect, investigate and prosecute offenders.

Further resources

Crime online is an emerging area, and there are often new articles coming out on crime on the internet. You might want to try reading some of this journal material to access ideas about contemporary debates and developments. Journals such as *Crime, Media, Culture and Criminology* and *Criminal Justice: An International Journal* are excellent sources. Try searching topics like internet and cybercrime in those journals and reading some recent articles.

There are a number of books on cybercrime, which is a growing area of criminological interest. However, one of the best remains Marjid Yars' (2006) *Cybercrime and Society*, which is an accessable and comprehensive introduction. David Wall's book *Cybercrime: The Transformation of Crime in the Information Age* (2007) is an exceptional text.

2.14   VICTIMOLOGY

Core Areas

Victimology

Early victimology

Labelling, victims and 'victimless crime'

Feminist criminology, domestic violence and victimization

Left realism and victimology

Repeat victimization

Right realism and victims

Critical victimology

Victims and restorative justice

RUNNING THEMES

Clearly the relationship between victim and offender is one of **power**, and victimology is concerned with this, but it is also concerned with the power relationship between the victim and the agencies of the state and the criminal justice system. The criminal justice system can further **discriminate** against victims of crime. Victimology is also concerned with **inequality**, and how factors such as **gender**, **class** and **race** can result in **inequality** in terms of the experience of victimization and the state response. Victimology similarly is linked to the study of people's perception of the likelihood of becoming a victim and the fear of crime, and therefore is also concerned with **representations** of crime.

KEY THINKER

John Braithwaite, in *Crime, Shame and Reintegration* (1989), put forward the suggestion that the key to crime control is a cultural commitment to what he termed 'reintegrative shaming' of lawbreakers. He suggests that some societies have higher crime rates than others because of the different processes of shaming wrong-doers. He accepts that shaming can be counterproductive, and can serve to increase crime problems, but suggests that when shaming is done within a cultural context of respect for the offender, it can be an extraordinarily powerful and efficient form of social control. Braithwaite's work is often regarded as the theoretical origins of 'restorative justice'.

VICTIMOLOGY

'Victimology' is the term that is used to detail the specific study of those who are the victims of crime. It was by the 1970s that academics began to be specifically concerned with the experiences of the victims of crime, and less concerned with relationships between victim and offender. Victimology is now sometimes regarded as a subdiscipline of criminology. It has developed significantly from attempts to map the characteristics of victims (in a similar fashion to that of early criminology and its attempts to map and define types of criminals) to focus upon the social and structural factors that influence the incidents and experience of victimization. Similarly, the background of researchers in the field of victimology has become more diverse, and in recent years victimology has drawn increasingly from feminist and critical criminology.

EARLY VICTIMOLOGY

Early criminological studies on victims sought to examine whether some people were more likely to be victims of crimes than others. More specifically, some sought to establish whether some responsibility for the crime lay with the victim, perhaps as a result of the victim's susceptibility to victimization, or the victim's participation in the events that led to the crime. Typically, these early positivistic research studies emphasized the ways that victims can contribute to their victimization. These studies created a climate within which policy-makers could obviate some of the responsibility for crime causation through a process of victim-blaming, but said little of the role of the state and its agencies.

Positivist victimology

Early victimology is often referred to as 'positivist victimology' because of the epistemology that informs it; however, not all criminologists use this term. If you see the term 'positivist victimology' it is likely that it is talking about early victimization studies.

Some examples of early victimology

- Hans Von Hentig's *The Criminal and the Victim* (1948) provided an analysis of the relationships between murderers and their victims by categorizing victims according to their behaviour and vulnerability. He argued that the victim was not a passive sufferer but that the victimization could be a result of the victim's own precipitation of, or proneness to, the crime.
- Wolfgang's *Patterns in Criminal Homicide* (1958) provided support for Von Hentig's argument. In a study of 588 murder cases in Philadelphia, Wolfgang concluded that in 26 per cent of the murders, the victims had 'initiated' the events that led to their death.
- Amir's study *Patterns of Forcible Rape* (1971) (like many studies subsequent to Wolfgang and Von Hentig) sought to apply the concept of victim precipitation to an inter-personal crime, and served to further 'blame the victim' (Amir's was perhaps the most controversial of early victim studies – he adopted a broader and more imprecise concept of 'victim precipitation' in an analysis of the victim–offender relationship in rape cases; the attribution of responsibility and blame to the victim in such cases has been strongly condemned). It should also be remembered that at the time of publication of Amir's study, feminists were starting to challenge his perspective, which they regarded as perpetuating the insidious myth that women invite rape (for example, by wearing the 'wrong' type of clothes or by walking down the 'wrong' unlit street).

It should be remembered that victim participation is not just an abstract theoretical concept, it is also evident in the justice process. Sexist and racist assumptions serve to undermine crimes such as rape and domestic violence and do little to explain victimization. For example, the murder of Stephen Lawrence highlighted how the police initially perceived Stephen (a young black male) to be in some way 'responsible' for his victimization. Due to the impact of feminism and more radical criminology, such bias assumptions have been challenged. However, it would be naïve to assume that such myth-driven racist (and sexist) assumptions do not continue to exist and examples of 'victim-blaming' are not still an intrinsic part of the criminal justice system and wider society.

LABELLING, VICTIMS AND 'VICTIMLESS CRIME'

The labelling of individuals as 'criminal' has attracted much debate and criticism but there has been little critical consideration of the meanings attached to or associated with the label 'victim'. It is often a pejorative, value-laden and problematic designation. Elsewhere feminists have rejected the label 'victim' as they regard it as stigmatizing and disempowering, preferring the term 'survivor' for those who have lived through sexual and physical abuse.

We should always attempt to avoid seeing 'criminals' and 'victims' as polar opposites, since we know that a great many criminals will have also experienced victimization. Indeed, in recent years a large body of work has suggested how the categories of criminal and victim often overlap.

In 1965 Edwin Schur wrote *Crimes Without Victims*, in which he discussed problems associated with the creation and enforcement of particular crimes including homosexuality, drug use and addiction, and abortion. He suggested that such offences were victimless, and simply involved the 'willing exchange, amongst adults, of strongly demanded but legally prohibited goods and services' (1965: 169). Schur suggested that laws which prohibited such types of behaviour created disrespect for the law. Similarly, when people fall into groups that are involved in such activities, they begin to form deviant identities. This identity could become so significant that it would eventually serve to prevent some individuals returning to the conventional world, even if they so desired.

The concept of *Crimes Without Victims* has now been widely challenged and has no real credibility, quite simply because crimes without victims do not exist. If we take drug addicts, for example, the victim may create costs for the state in terms of treatment, or may be unable to engage in a legitimate occupation due to their addiction. Others would suggest that the addict, or their family, can be construed as the victim, and more still would point to the way in which the drug trade is based upon violence and victimization in a broader sense.

FEMINIST CRIMINOLOGY, DOMESTIC VIOLENCE AND VICTIMIZATION

During the 1970s the women's movement began to draw attention to the suffering of women in the private sphere (largely in the home). However, Wright and Hill (2004) have highlighted how at that time the problem was understood largely in terms of the victims' own inadequate personalities. This was often because it was the male professionals who were explaining domestic violence. Many criminal justice professionals asked why women in violent relationships did not leave their violent partners. They implied that it was not only irrational for women to stay, but that because they did, they were responsible for their own continued victimization. Feminist researchers, on the other hand, began to point to the very rational reasons why women stayed in violent relationships. They did this by shifting from a positivist approach to an interpretivist approach, where they engaged more with those who had experienced victimization and generated knowledge about what it is like to be an abused woman, much of which confounded rather than confirmed traditional views.

LEFT REALISM AND VICTIMOLOGY

The break with left idealism that resulted in left realism was, as you have already seen (in Chapter 2.5) largely due to the concern that left idealism did not take crime or the experiences of victimization as seriously as it should. Therefore, early left realist crime surveys underscored the way in which those who were socially excluded suffered more greatly the ill effects of crime (the poor, ethnic minorities and women suffered the most).

The left realist approach fixes the victim in the equation of the 'square of crime' a model which explains the crime rate as a consequence of the interaction between the agencies of social control, such as the state, the offender, the public and the victim. In this way, left realists tried to avoid the positivist tendency to indulge in victim-blaming (see Chapter 2.5).

The concept of the 'square of crime' minimizes any division between victim and offender and maximizes the sense that crime involves a relationship. For left realists, the impact of crime and victimization depends upon, among other things, the response by state agencies such as the police and the courts. A consequence of inappropriate or unsympathetic responses from such agencies, for instance, if a victim-blaming response is evident, the result is further stigmatization of the victim, often referred to as 'secondary victimization'. This is an important concept as it highlights the way in which it is not only the criminal act that does harm – the response to the criminal act from state agencies can also be harmful to the victim.

Secondary victimization is a concept that stems from left realist criminology. It describes how victims can be victimized by the primary criminal offence, and then revictimized by the acts or omissions of the criminal justice system.

REPEAT VICTIMIZATION

Simply put, repeat victimization (RV) is the recurrence of crime in the same places and/or against the same people. The target can be an individual, a group of persons, a property or another crime target. Repeat victimization can be by either the same or a different offender, and can involve the same or different types of crime. The traditional Home Office definition (Bridgeman and Hobbs, 1997) is that repeat victimization occurs '... when the same person or place suffers from more than one incident over a specified period of time'.

Repeat offending has a voluminous literature, and grew influential as a concept from the 1990s with the growth of administrative criminology and routine activity theories. The body of work on repeat victimization is still growing, and preventing repeat victimization is emerging as an important area for policing and crime control. One of the first traceable studies of repeat victimization was by Johnson and colleagues; it examined hospital staff observations about the frequency with which some people returned to a Texas hospital with serious gunshot and stab wounds. Their concern was orientated toward the implied drain upon hospital resources and the possible implications for health insurance practices (Johnson et al., 1973).

In the UK as a concept it is often associated with the work of administrative criminologists such as Ken Pease and Graham Farrell, who produced pioneering work on the topic in the early 1990s. Indeed as a concept RV is tied to policy applications, and has been the basis, for example, of giving crime prevention advice to victims as a means of preventing repeat instances of crime.

RIGHT REALISM AND VICTIMS

Although right realists have little to say about the experience of victimization, their political philosophy is one of deterrence and punishment. Therefore without any real focus upon the experience of victimization they have promoted more punitive, deterrent interventions. More recently, some criminologists have questioned the role that victimology can play in proving the justification required by the political right to introduce harsher sentences for perpetrators. An example is how Michael Howard's 'prison works' speech in 1993 was followed shortly afterwards by promises to put victims at the centre of the criminal justice process. These approaches often boil down to a simplistic equation where increased rights for the victim equal greater losses for the offender.

CRITICAL VICTIMOLOGY

Critical victimology essentially takes its lead from critical criminology, with which it shares common features, but emphasizes that victimization is associated with structural powerlessness. This view of victimization recognizes that the impact of criminal victimization is made more complex by factors such as age, sex and race. Critical victimology, due to its reliance upon notions such as 'patriarchy', shared a concern with highlighting the hidden and complex nature of some forms of victimization (for example, the abuse of children and the elderly). As a concept it is associated with Mawby and Walklate's (1994) book, *Critical Victimology*. A critical approach to the issue of victimization looks to the structure of society in which those crimes take place and asks uncomfortable questions about the adequacy of the response by the state for some victims. The low levels of policing and prosecution relating to some types of crime (such as corporate crime and crime that occurs in the private sphere) suggest that the criminal justice system itself is complicit in further victimizing individuals. This is an important point since it challenges the ideological view that 'get tough' approaches can be justified on the grounds that they demonstrate the willingness of the state to take the needs of victims seriously.

VICTIMS AND RESTORATIVE JUSTICE

Restorative justice is a concept that has only really gained momentum in recent years, but has had a quite profound impact upon criminology and more specifically victimology.

In *Crime, Shame and Reintegration* (1989), John Braithwaite attempted to outline an alternative strategy that promoted a radically different criminal justice policy, based upon models where reintegrative shaming forms the model for punishing transgressions of society's rules. Framing his work particularly around the justice of Aborigines in Australia, he argued that low crime societies were those that successfully balanced shame for the offender's actions with a concern for individual support and validation for that person. Braithwaite has proved influential in academic argument and contributed to a growing momentum for criminal justice practice based upon 'restorative justice' principles.

There is a wide range of definitions of what 'restorative justice' involves, but regardless of the specifics of definition, it tends to equate with making amends, paying back, forgiveness and moving forward, making restorative justice in the most part a 'peacemaking' approach. One of the most commonly accepted definitions in Britain suggests that 'Restorative Justice is a process whereby parties with a stake in a specific offence collectively resolve how to deal with the aftermath of the offence and its implication for the future' (Marshall, 1999).

In the 1990s, the term 'restorative justice' came to be applied to a wide range of ideas and practices in criminal justice systems, and those schemes that unite victim, offender and community, which exist across a range of societies. That stated, as definitions tend to vary, a bewildering and diverse range of programmes and schemes have been placed under the banner of 'restorative justice'. This is in part because restorative justice owes much of its appeal to the fact that it promotes inclusive roles for those often neglected in the criminal justice process, bringing both victims and offenders to the centre stage. Therefore the development of restorative justice should be considered part of a wider strategy to include victims in the criminal justice process.

While restorative justice has had a number of fierce advocates, in one of the few texts to examine the more negative aspects of a restorative approach, Declan Roche suggested that 'for all its promise of promoting healing and harmony, restorative justice can deliver a justice as cruel and vengeful as any' (2003: 1). Part of the problem is that due to differences in definition, and ideological disagreements regarding concepts such as shame, there exist fundamental differences in individuals' views about what restoration should involve. Should offenders be *made* to feel 'guilt' for their acts, or *forced* to say sorry?

Common pitfall

There are some fierce advocates of restorative approaches, but there are fewer accounts that really criticize restorative justice. Try not to fall into the trap of regarding restorative justice as a 'solution' to the problem of crime.

You might want to try answering this question as if it were a 45 minute written exam question.

"A restorative justice scheme calls a conference which was convened for a 12-year-old boy caught shoplifting. The proposal of his mother that he should stand outside the shop wearing a T-shirt emblazoned with the words 'I am a thief' all day on a Saturday was agreed with the store manager. Do you think this is a good idea? How can you support your answer with criminological theory?"

You can address this question using an 'advantages and disadvantages' approach (see Part 3). Use the information in this section on restorative justice as a guide, however, you should not forget that labelling/interactionist theory could also be used here. What might be the negative aspects of such an intervention? Is Schur right to argue that it might be better to do nothing? How is the young person going to experience reintegration rather than simply shame alone?

Further resources

Although the concept of victim-precipitation was supposedly designed to provide a value-neutral explanation of victimization, we have seen that such neutrality does not exist and that we need to question the values upon which some judgements are made. As you will now be aware, it has often been women who have been held responsible for inviting victimization, whereas men have not. Whether someone is constructed as 'blameless' or 'culpable', and is viewed as either a 'worthy' or 'unworthy' 'victim', often depends upon sexist, racist or class-based assumptions.

Davies, Francis and Greer's (2007) book, *Victims, Crime and Society* is an excellent edited collection that comprehensively covers a range of core subject areas and victim groups. Walklate's (2007) *Handbook of Victims and Victimology* is a useful text. Davies' *Gender, Crime and Victimization* (2010) is an interesting examination of these two intertwined areas that is not as dated as some of the other texts.

PART THREE

STUDY, WRITING AND REVISION SKILLS

Chapters

3.1   GENERAL INTRODUCTION

Success in any course will not simply come about by developing knowledge of theory; instead you will need to be able to demonstrate that you have a comprehensive grasp of the subject matter, and that you can apply theory.

To this end, university degrees and criminology courses are likely to require some form of assessment. It is true to suggest that ultimately the knowledge that you gain as part of a degree course is only one part of the learning experience. If you are successful on a university degree course you will acquire an array of transferable skills that will assist you in gaining employment.

Therefore, this book intends to combine theoretical knowledge of criminology with useful practical guidance about how to undertake study. If you work your way through this chapter you should, at the end, be better equipped to profit from your lectures, benefit from your seminars, construct your essays efficiently, develop effective revision strategies and respond comprehensively to the pressures of exam situations.

Finally, it may be worth thinking about treating study skills as a separate area for you to read around, especially in the early stages of your studies. Some universities will have a module designed to improve your study skills at the early stages of your course, but whether this is available to you or not, I recommend that you obtain and read a copy of Harrison et al.'s book *Study Skills for Criminology* (2012) alongside this chapter.

In the six sections that lie ahead you will be presented with:

- checklists and bullet points to focus your attention on key issues
- exercises to help you participate actively in the learning experience
- illustrations and analogies to enable you to anchor learning principles in everyday events and experiences
- worked examples to demonstrate the use of such features as structure, headings and continuity
- tips that provide practical advice that will benefit you in your study of criminology.

There are also a number of self directed exercises in this section that have been devised to try and get you to practise techniques and skills that will be useful for you. You should decide how much effort you would like to invest in each exercise, according to your individual preferences and requirements.

Finally, the overall aim of Part 3 is to direct you to the key points for academic and personal development. The twin emphases of academic development and personal qualities are stressed throughout. By giving attention to these factors you will give yourself the attributes you will need to succeed in your studies.

3.2   DEALING WITH THEORY

This section will help you to:

- recognize the importance of engaging with social theory
- display the ability to think critically about 'social theory'
- be able to test theories against six criteria.

As you will now be aware, criminology is a theoretical discipline, and therefore you will be expected to be able to engage more generally with 'social theory'. As you will also be aware, criminologists will often hold differing opinions about where criminology should be most closely connected. Some undergraduate criminology programmes are delivered in departments of law, sociology, social policy or political studies. I see criminology as a social science that is closely allied with sociology, and I believe that criminology cannot be separated from social theory, as it is undoubtedly concerned with problems of social order and disorder. A look at the classic texts that influence criminology, for example, Marx, Durkheim, and the Chicago School, clearly shows the way that criminology and social theory are deeply interwoven. I therefore believe that it is imperative that students of criminology are able to engage with and understand social theory. To that end, and to assist you in developing as a criminologist, I intend to begin by giving you some guidance about how to deal with 'theory' generally, and more specifically how you can go about 'evaluating' and thinking critically about social theory.

SIX CRITERIA FOR EVALUATING THEORY

It is not the case that to achieve success in criminology you must simply passively learn information and learn to repeat what you have been told. Instead, most courses will expect students to develop 'critical insight' or 'critical thinking'. This does not mean that they want or expect students to readily criticize everything that they encounter, rather they want you to consider the information that you receive, and consider what is good and what is bad, that you use the evidence and arguments that you encounter to form opinions, and that you use evidence to support assertions that you make. Essentially what is meant by these terms is that students are expected to have a comprehensive and informed knowledge, where opinions are formed by understanding drawn from a range of sources.

To help you develop critical thinking skills in criminology you will have to show that you can critique and scrutinize theory. To that end you might want to use the criteria presented below to assist you. You do not have to take a criminological theory and subject it to each criteria as a test, but rather regard these criteria as a set of guidelines that you can choose from when you encounter theory. They are intended to help you to display an ability to analyse and offer insightful comment, for example, you might talk about the potential applicability of biological criminology, such as eugenics or genetic engineering.

Criteria 1 – Logical consistency

Logical consistency is about whether a theory makes sense; essentially, is it clear? This means asking questions such as: Does a theory use clearly defined concepts? Does it use clearly defined relationships between concepts? (We call these propositions.) Essentially, does it make sense?

Criteria 2 – Scope

The concept of scope refers to whether there is clarity about the range of events, trends or facts that the theory intends to explain. For example, is it a theory that seeks to explain all crime, just some types of crimes, or perhaps only one type of crime? Is it a theory that applies in different places (perhaps one town, city or country)? For example, Robert Merton's concept of criminal innovation in 'strain theory' only really deals with crime which is financially motivated, and not all crime is.

Criteria 3 – Parsimony

The term 'parsimony' literally means thriftiness or stinginess, but here it is used to make the assertion that any theoretical explanation should be as well-organized and well-argued as possible. The theory should not use more concepts and propositions than are necessary. The idea is that theory should use as few propositions as possible in order to explain the widest range of occurrence.

Criteria 4 – Testability

A theory must be tested against facts. It is not scientific if it cannot be 'verified' or 'falsified' by appropriate reportable and observable evidence. To describe this reportable and observable evidence, we use the term 'empirical'. A theory must be framed in such a way that its propositions are 'falsifiable' – meaning it must be possible, in principle, to prove it wrong. In criminology a good theory is one that is not proven wrong, as social scientists think it impossible to prove something 'absolutely true'.

Any theory, even if the evidence seems to fit, is only ever 'provisionally true'. This is as close as social scientists get to verification. A better theory or a better understanding and interpretation of the perceived facts may one day supersede it. This is especially true in social sciences!

Criteria 5 – Empirical validity

Empirical validity is concerned with whether a theory is supported by research evidence. If it is not, is it making grand claims with no evidence, or is it a hypothesis that needs further consideration? If it is based upon research we need to consider carefully how the research was gathered. Did more than one researcher produce the research? In more than one place? Was the research process undertaken over time or all at once? We need to consider whether the core principles that inform the research are falsified/proven wrong. Just because a theory isn't supported or tested empirically doesn't make it a bad theory (there are a number of criminological theories that cannot be empirically tested) but may serve to limit its usefulness in terms of application (see below).

Criteria 6 – Usefulness and applicability

I use this term because, as stated earlier, criminological theory can underpin, and be used to inform, criminal justice policy, interventions and practices. This criteria is concerned with describing how easily the theory can be turned into criminal justice policy and practice, but criminal justice policy-making is not simply based on rational, i.e. good, empirically grounded theory, but is likely to be based on a mix of ideological, cultural, economic and political considerations.

> Moral principles and beliefs about how people should treat one another, for example, how society should treat offenders, should inform and influence the development of criminal justice policy. We should not be wholly influenced by what is effective and what seems to work, and policy and practice should not be determined by evidence of effectiveness alone. As an extreme example, if we found that cutting people's limbs off, or executing them for theft worked better than anything else, we might still want to argue that it is not morally the right thing to do.

Having begun to think about critically considering the theoretical material that you will encounter on your criminology course, it is now time to turn our attention to how, practically, you can make the most of the opportunities that are presented to you during undergraduate study. The following sections are intended as a guide to how you can achieve more from your study.

3.3 HOW TO GET THE MOST OUT OF YOUR LECTURES

This chapter will help you to:

- make the most of your lecture notes
- prepare your mind for new terms
- develop an independent approach to learning
- write efficient summary notes from lectures
- take the initiative in building on your lectures.

KEEPING IN CONTEXT

According to leading higher educational commentators and advisors, best quality learning is facilitated when it is set within an overall learning context. It should be the responsibility of your tutors to provide a context for you to learn in, but it is also your responsibility to contribute to this overall environment, and you can do this even before your first lecture begins.

The demands of higher education are quite different, and much of the work that you undertake at university is self-directed, that is to say that students take responsibility for managing much of the process of their own learning. Subjects like criminology are vast, with a great deal written by leading scholars and intellectuals, and the idea that you can master the subject from reading a single text that will tell you all you need to know is an absolute fallacy. In order to progress you will get guidance in subject areas from academic staff in the shape of lectures. However, in the restricted hours of a lecture it is impossible for even the best teacher to cover anything more than the core areas. In a way what the lecturer does is provide an aerial map of the ground, but it will be your task to familiarize yourself with much of the specifics of the streets and know not only general information but to look at the subjects themselves in more detail.

You can, and should, develop an overview of the subject matter before you ever attend a lecture, and this is why you will be given a module guide or course handbook that contains details of your programme of study and lectures. Such guidance is given to students to read, but I am often surprised that students do not see these documents as essential reading. Preparing adequately for lectures is the first way to ensure that you get the most out of them, and toward this your first task should always be to know what is coming up in your lectures and prepare yourself before you enter the lecture. This can be achieved by becoming familiar with the outline content of a given subject and the entire study programme, doing preparatory reading and preparing yourself before you set foot in a lecture theatre. Before you go into each lecture you should briefly remind yourself of where it fits into the overall scheme of things. Think, for example, of how more confident you feel when you move into a new city (e.g. to attend university) once you become familiar with your surroundings, i.e. where you live in relation to college, shops, stores, stations, places of entertainment. The same is true of criminology, and some of the preparation you should be involved in is keeping abreast of relevant developments in the criminal justice system. Apart from reading the study materials and course books, you should spend some time thinking about how you develop a comprehensive general knowledge about crime and criminal justice. For example, using good quality news media to keep up to date with social and political developments relating to criminal justice is an important aspect of the background preparatory work you should be doing throughout your criminology course. While reading textbooks is important, you may want to watch higher quality news programming, read good broadsheet newspapers and listen to relevant radio broadcasts and podcasts.

The benefit of reading and engaging in this way is that you will develop relevant knowledge that will no doubt help you in discussions and assessments. The important thing to remember is that only so much can be covered during the course, and the most successful students will take an active interest in the topic beyond what is expected in modules and as the core course content. In becoming more familiar generally with the subject you will find that you engage better with the specifics of the course you study and begin to see the bigger picture. Beyond that, criminology is not simply an academic subject, but is a real world one. Keeping abreast of real world developments is vital.

USE OF LECTURE NOTES

It is always beneficial to do some preliminary reading before you enter a lecture. If lecture notes are provided in advance (for example, electronically), then print these out, read over them and bring them with you to the lecture. You can insert question marks on issues where you will need further clarification. Some lecturers prefer to provide full notes, some prefer to make skeleton outlines available and some prefer to issue no notes at all. Whichever the style of lecturer, some basic preparation will equip you with a great advantage – you will be able to 'tune in' and think more clearly about the lecture than you would have done without the preliminary work. So too reading and preparing for lectures will help you get much more out of the content, as will following up on lectures by undertaking further self-directed study.

I have also found that often students do not really think about what they record and take down as lecture notes, as often they become involved in attempting to write material that they are provided with or which is covered in chapters in books, but fail to take down the names of theorists, works and sources of further reading that are suggested in the class. It is worth remembering what notes are for: they are taken as an aid to memory and a guide to further reading. It therefore stands to reason that you will probably not have to note down everything. Instead try to actively listen and think discerningly about what you are writing as notes, rather than simply becoming involved in writing down what the lecturer is saying for the sake of it.

> You ought to spend some time thinking about how and why you go about making lecture notes. What purpose will they serve? I would suggest that they are often best used as a means of navigating the subject on your own. If you take down everything said in a lecture you may not get the most from it. I always suggest that students make pertinent notes, such as authors' names and any books mentioned. I would suggest that this will almost certainly be the case if notes are supplied to accompany the lecture.

MASTERING TECHNICAL TERMS

Let us assume that in an early lecture you are introduced to a series of new terms such as 'paradigm', 'recidivism', 'empirical' and 'hegemony'. If you are hearing these and other terms for the first time, you could end up with a headache! New words can be threatening, especially if you have to face a string of them in one lecture. The uncertainty about the new terms may impair your ability to benefit fully from the lecture and therefore affect the quality of your learning. Some subjects require technical terms and the use of them is unavoidable. However, when you have heard a term a number of times it will not seem as daunting as it initially was.

In terms of learning new words, it will be very useful if you can work out what they mean from their context when you first encounter them. You might be much better at this than you imagine, especially if there is only one word in the sentence that you do not understand. It would also be very useful if you could obtain a small indexed notebook and use this to build up your own glossary of terms. In this way you could include a definition of a word, an example of its use, where it fits into a theory and any practical application of it.

To develop your learning it is worth investing some time in developing your vocabulary. To this end you should buy a good dictionary (this will also help you when you encounter terms you are unsure of). To progress in your study of criminology I would also suggest purchasing a dictionary of sociology – these are available at a reasonable price and offer definitions of many of the core terms you will encounter in criminology. Similarly the *Sage Dictionary of Criminology* is also a useful resource.

Remember you can also extend your vocabulary by reading a broad range of material that will help you to learn new words, and this may improve your ability to write generally.

Reading broadsheet newspapers, for example, will benefit you two-fold: it will assist you in developing your writing, while it will also extend your knowledge of the practices of the criminal justice system that will form the backdrop to academic criminology.

Checklist: Mastering terms used in your lectures

- ✓ Read lecture notes before the lectures and list any unfamiliar terms.
- ✓ Read over the listed terms until you are familiar with their sound.
- ✓ Try to work out meanings of terms from their context.
- ✓ Write out a sentence that includes the new word (do this for each word).
- ✓ Meet up with other students and test each other with the technical terms.
- ✓ Note down any new words that you hear in lectures and check out the meaning soon afterwards.
- ✓ Do not be afraid to ask if you do not understand something.
- ✓ Try to expand your vocabulary and learn new words.
- ✓ Invest in a dictionary of key terms – the *Sage Dictionary of Criminology* is a useful purchase and the glossary section of this book may help.

NOTE-TAKING STRATEGY

Note-taking in lectures is an art that you will only perfect with practice and by trial and error. You should not feel that you cannot ignore my opinions if you find an alternative formula that works best for you. What works for one, does not always work for all. Some students can write more quickly than others, some are better at shorthand than others and some are better at deciphering their own scrawl! The problem will always be to try to find a balance between concentrating beneficially on what you hear, and making sufficient notes that will enable you to later comprehend what you have heard. You should not, however, become frustrated by the fact that you will not immediately understand or remember everything you have heard.

It should be remembered that lectures really only deliver the bare bones of the subject, the essential points or a potted history. It is difficult to condense expansive subjects into the space of an hour or two, and many of the topics of the lectures you will attend will be the subject of a plethora of books and articles in their own right. A mistake too many people make is associating the lecture with the sum total of what you have to do, and students often make the mistake of thinking that in attending the lecture, they have done all that is required of them. The key lesson I would want to impart is that the lecture should be the beginning of the learning process, not the sum total of it. However, it will be an important part of helping you plan a route round the subject and the key components. Therefore, attending lectures is important, whether it is a requirement of your course or not.

> By being present at a lecture you will already have an advantage over students who do not attend. The notes that you take will undoubtedly benefit you further, but I would urge you to consider why you take notes and how you will use them. By stopping and asking yourself this, and reflecting on it, it is likely that you will produce more useful notes.

SOME GUIDELINES FOR NOTE-TAKING IN LECTURES

- Develop the note-taking strategy that works best for you.
- Work at finding a balance between listening and writing.
- Make some use of optimal shorthand (for example, a few key words may summarize a story).

- Too much writing may impair the flow of the lecture for you.
- Too much writing may impair the quality of your notes.
- Some limited notes are better than none.
- Good note-taking may facilitate deeper processing of information.
- It is essential to 'tidy up' notes as soon as possible after a lecture.
- Reading over notes soon after lectures will consolidate your learning.

DEVELOPING THE LECTURE

Lectures are not just a passive experience

- Try to interact with the lecture material by asking questions.
- Highlight points that you would like to develop in personal study.
- Trace connections between the lecture and other parts of your study programme.
- Bring together notes from the lecture and other sources.
- Restructure the lecture outline into your own preferred format.
- Think of ways in which aspects of the lecture material can be applied.
- Design ways in which aspects of the lecture material can be illustrated.
- If the lecturer invites questions, make a note of all the questions asked.
- Follow up on issues of interest that have arisen out of the lecture.

3.4   HOW TO GET THE MOST OUT OF YOUR SEMINARS

This chapter will help you to:

- be aware of the value of seminars
- focus on links to learning
- recognize qualities you can use repeatedly
- manage potential problems in seminars
- prepare yourself adequately for seminars
- find, read and use academic journal articles.

NOT TO BE UNDERESTIMATED

Seminars are often optional in a degree programme and sometimes are poorly attended because their value is underestimated. Some students may be convinced that the lecture is the truly authoritative way to receive quality information. Undoubtedly, lectures play an important role in an academic programme, but seminars have a unique contribution to learning that will complement lectures. Other students may feel that their time would be better spent in personal study. Again, private study is unquestionably essential for personal learning and development, but you will nevertheless diminish your learning experience if you neglect seminars. If seminars were to be removed from academic programmes, then something really important would be lost.

Most seminars are intended to be an interactive experience where students are more actively involved in the learning process, although different university institutions may have different conventions such as workshops, group sessions and debate forums. Whatever the system at the institution you are at, your study should include some active involvement in the learning process rather than passively being taught subject essentials in a lecture environment. It is really important that you use this opportunity, and it is important that you prepare, come willing to participate and get involved. This will not only aid your own learning, it will make for a more vibrant and effective learning environment generally and improve the skills you have.

AN ASSET TO COMPLEMENT OTHER LEARNING ACTIVITIES

Seminars will provide you with a unique opportunity to learn and develop. At university, it is in seminars that you will hear a variety of contributions, and different perspectives and emphases. You will have the chance to interrupt and the experience of being interrupted! You will also learn that you can get things wrong! It is often the case that when one student admits that they did not know some important piece of information, other students quickly follow on to the same admission in the wake of this. If you can learn to ask questions and not feel stupid, then seminars will give you an asset for learning and a life-long educational quality.

CREATING THE RIGHT CLIMATE IN SEMINARS

In lectures your main role is to listen and take notes, but in seminars there is the challenge to strike the balance between listening and speaking. It is important to make a beginning in speaking even if it is just to repeat something that you agree with. However, seminars are only one aspect of the learning process. If you are committed to independent learning you will have more to offer other students if you work in small groups, and you will also be prompted to follow up on the leads given by them. Furthermore, the guidelines given to you in lectures are designed to lead you into deeper independent study. The issues raised in lectures are pointers to provide direction and structure for your extended personal pursuit. Your aim should invariably be to build on what you are given, and you should never think of merely returning the bare bones of the lecture material in a course work essay or exam.

It almost never fails to impress tutors and markers if you show a contemporary knowledge of the subject that expands upon the content of the course and shows an ability to gather evidence beyond the material covered in the course. Use journals to search for relevant studies that may be cited in exams and essays.

HOW TO FIND, READ AND USE ACADEMIC JOURNAL ARTICLES

When conducting your own research and when directing your own studies you will often encounter dozens of possibilities in your search for material that might be relevant reading, and might prove useful for your studies. Often you will get a comprehensive recommended reading list, and books obtained from university libraries will no doubt prove useful. However, the most up–to-date and recent material you will encounter may well come in the form of academic journal articles.

Academic journals are periodicals in which researchers publish articles on their work. Most often these articles discuss recent research. Journals also publish theoretical discussions and articles that critically review already published work. The best academic journals are typically peer-reviewed, meaning that in order to have something printed in them, an academic's work must be reviewed (often in an anonymous process) by two colleagues. The process is meant to make sure that only the best, clear, well-written and rigorously researched articles are published. On the whole, the process can work well, but while some articles are useful, some will be very niche, and occasionally some are full of jargon and can be almost entirely incomprehensible. However, if you use journal articles properly, you can develop knowledge of very up-to-date debates and issues that will be relevant to your studies and will aid you in assessments.

When it comes to using journal articles and searching them out there are a number of search engines that can help you identify potentially relevant articles. Sage criminology, for example, gives access to the full collection of Sage journals, and there are a number of ways to search using it. However, even when you find articles that seem relevant in terms of title, you still need to look a little further. Beyond the title most articles will have what is called an abstract. This is a short paragraph at the start of the article which summarizes the theme and topic of the article and says what it concerns. Therefore it is wise to read the abstract first – article titles often always give much information, and similarly searches may pick up keywords but bring forward articles that are not really relevant to your interest. The abstract should give you just enough information to let you know the basics of the article. From this you will know whether you should read on or look elsewhere for your project. Some journals print a list of keywords pertaining to the article as well. Learning which articles will be useful, and those which are only of tangential relevance is a skill, but it is a skill you will develop as you progress in your studies.

LINKS IN LEARNING AND TRANSFERABLE SKILLS

An important principle in the progression from shallow to deep learning is developing the capacity to make connecting links between themes or topics and across subjects. This also applies to the various learning activities such as lectures, seminars, fieldwork, computer searches and private study. Another factor to think about is the skills you can develop, or improve on, from seminars that you can use across your study programme. A couple of examples of key skills are the ability to communicate and the capacity to work within a team. These are skills that you will be able to use at various points in your course (they are transferable), but you are not likely to develop them within the formal setting of a lecture.

> It is worth remembering that these skills are also transferable to the world of work, and many of the skills that you will use at university will be highly sought after by employers. Think about how what you have done at university might mirror skills that employers may ask for.

In each seminar that you attend you should be looking for links between subjects and the broader themes. If you are studying a module-based course, it is likely that topics covered in some modules will link and complement other modules. Look for these links to maximize the value of each and every seminar.

AN OPPORTUNITY TO CONTRIBUTE

If you have never made a contribution to a seminar before, you may need something to use as an 'ice breaker'. It does not matter if your first contribution is only a sentence or two – the important thing is to make a start. One way to do this is to make brief notes as others contribute, and whilst doing this a question or two might arise in your mind. If your first contribution is a question, that is a good start. Or it may be that you will be able to point out some connection between what others have said, or identify conflicting opinions that need to be resolved. If you have already begun making contributions, it is important that you keep the momentum going, and do not allow yourself to lapse back into the safe cocoon of shyness.

STRATEGIES FOR BENEFITING FROM YOUR SEMINAR EXPERIENCE

If you are required to do a presentation in your seminar, you might want to consult a full chapter on presentations in a complementary study guide. Alternatively, you may be content with the summary bullet points presented as a checklist below. In order to benefit from discussions in seminars (the focus of this chapter), the following may be useful.

Checklist: How to benefit from seminars

- ✓ Do some preparatory reading.
- ✓ Familiarize yourself with the main ideas to be addressed.
- ✓ Make notes during the seminar.
- ✓ Make some verbal contribution, even a question.
- ✓ Remind yourself of the skills you can develop.
- ✓ Trace learning links from the seminar to other subjects/topics on your programme.

✓ Make brief bullet points on what you should follow up.
✓ Read over your notes as soon as possible after the seminar.
✓ Continue discussion with fellow students after the seminar has ended.

3.5   ESSAY WRITING TIPS

This chapter will help you to:

- quickly engage with the main arguments
- channel your passions constructively
- note your main arguments in an outline
- find and focus on your central topic questions
- weave quotations into your essay
- know about plagiarism and avoid it.

GETTING INTO THE FLOW

In essay writing one of your first aims should be to get your mind active and engaged with your subject. A former teacher of mine used to say 'practice makes better!' which I find a good tonic to the idea that 'perfection' is attainable. Just as professional sportspeople will practise their skills, and 'warm up' before an event, you can 'warm up' for your essay. Practice will make you better, and reflecting on ideas in your head before you begin to write will allow you to think within the framework of your topic, and this will be especially important if you are coming to the subject for the first time.

THE TRIBUTARY PRINCIPLE

A tributary is a stream that runs into a main river as it wends its way to the sea. Similarly in an essay you should ensure that every idea you introduce is moving toward the overall theme you are addressing. Your idea might of course be relevant to a subheading that is in turn relevant to a main heading. Every idea you introduce is to be a 'feeder' into the flowing theme. In addition to tributaries, there can also be 'distributaries', which are streams that flow away from the river. In an essay, these would represent the ideas that run away from the main stream of thought and leave the reader trying to work out what their relevance may have been. It is one thing to have grasped your subject thoroughly, but quite another to convince your reader that this is the case. Your aim should be to build up ideas sentence by sentence and paragraph by paragraph, until you have communicated your clear purpose to the reader.

It is important in essay writing that you do not include material that is irrelevant. It is also important that you make linking statements – these will convey to the reader that you have made the link. Also, explain how what you are using contributes to your discussion and why it is relevant.

Many students do not achieve their full potential in essays, and often this is because they fail to prepare enough or to undertake enough background work to properly prepare. I often say to students that it is vital that they feel that they have a good understanding of the subject before they start, and they should be able to have a confident conversation about the subject matter where they can discuss the key standpoints and theoretical contributions on the subject before they even start writing. Unfortunately, many still fall into the trap of knowing little and commencing their essay with their books at their side and a lack of clarity on what they will be writing about. It is always better to start on a confident footing, and while I would not expect students to be able to recite every detail before they commence work on an assessment, my suspicion is that it is those who fail to prepare sufficiently that tend to find essay writing most difficult.

LISTING AND LINKING THE KEY CONCEPTS

All subjects will have central concepts that can sometimes be usefully labelled by a single word. Course textbooks may include a glossary of terms and these provide a direct route to the beginning of efficient mastery of the topic. The central words or terms are the essential raw materials that you will need to build upon. Ensure that you learn the words and their definitions, and that you can go on to link the key words together, so that in your learning activities you will add understanding. The glossary in this book should help you toward this goal.

AN ADVERSARIAL SYSTEM

In higher education students are required to make the transition from descriptive to critical writing. If you can think of the critical approach as a law case that is being conducted where there is both a prosecution and a defence, your concern should be for objectivity, transparency and fairness. No matter how passionately you may feel about a given cause you must not allow information to be filtered out because of your personal prejudice. An essay is not to become a crusade for a cause in which the contrary arguments are not addressed in an even-handed manner. This means that you should show awareness that opposite views are held and you should at least represent these as accurately as possible.

> In many ways your role as a writer is to play judge; you assess all the evidence presented, and then come to a decision on that basis. That is not too say that you cannot have an opinion or make a conclusion that you feel is appropriate, but you must give both sides of an argument a fair hearing!

STIRRING UP PASSIONS

The above points do not of course mean that you are not entitled to personal persuasion or to feel passionately about your subject. On the contrary, such feelings may well be a marked advantage if you can bring them under control and channel them into balanced, effective writing (see example below). Some students may be struggling at the other end of the spectrum – being required to write about a topic that they feel quite indifferent about. As you engage with your topic and toss the ideas around in your mind, you will hopefully find that your interest is stimulated, if only at an intellectual level initially. How strongly you feel about a topic or how much you are interested in it may depend on whether you choose the topic yourself or whether it has been given to you as an obligatory assignment.

AN EXAMPLE OF AN ISSUE THAT MAY STIR UP PASSIONS

Table 3.1   Should a sentence of life imprisonment for murder mean life?

For	Against
• It would be a strong form of 'incapacitation'	• There is no proof of deterrent effect, as many murders would still happen
• The general deterrent effect	• Miscarriages of justice can and do occur
• Individual deterrent effect	• Such a punishment could be unjust in implementation
• Such sentences might provide justice for victims	• The existing system of life imprisonment is effective

For	Against
• Freed life-sentenced prisoners have killed again	• Prisoners serving natural life have 'nothing to lose' in prison
• There are already natural life prisoners in Britain	• Such a sentence panders to popular punitiveness
• By using utilitarian principles, it can be argued that the rights of the individual are outweighed by the greater good of the public who are being protected	• The prison population would increase
	• The resultant ageing prison population creates problems with regard to a care/control balance, as it has in America and the UK
	• Such an approach gives no credit to the possibility of reform or treatment

STRUCTURING AN OUTLINE

Whenever you sense a flow of inspiration to write on a given subject, it is essential that you put this into a structure that will allow your inspiration to be communicated clearly. It is a basic principle in all walks of life that structure and order facilitate good communication. Therefore, when you have the flow of inspiration in your essay you must get this into a structure that will allow the marker to recognize the true quality of your work. For example, you might plan for an introduction, conclusion, three main headings and each of these with several subheadings (see example overleaf). Moreover, you may decide not to include your headings in your final presentation, i.e. just use them initially to structure and balance your arguments. Once you have drafted this outline you can then easily sketch an introduction, and you will have been well prepared for the conclusion when you arrive at that point.

Common pitfall

Students who achieve lower marks often lack focus in their work. A good structure will help you to achieve a balance in the weight of each of your arguments, while a good essay plan will also support you toward this goal. Also, remember that preparation is one vital aspect of presentation, but so is proof-reading and accuracy checking: you should spend a sizeable amount of time rereading what you have written for presentation, grammar, clarity, accuracy, etc.

The example below gives an outline structure that you could use to write a purposeful essay. The topic is one relevant to criminology and the authors named can be traced and read if you want to practise researching and writing an essay. Again this is only one approach that you could take (there is never a right answer).

How have academic criminologists sought to explain serial killing as a phenomenon?

1 Defining serial murder

    i. Defining serial murder is very complex and contested (Coleman and Norris, 2000)

    ii. We may know very little as to the extent of such a phenomenon (Kiger, 1990)

    iii. Serial murder may be increasing, and this may be due to social influences and factors (Leyton, 1989)

    iv. We have a duty to try to find explanations; and these may assist in locating and identifying perpetrators, and protecting victims often drawn from vulnerable communities (Wilson, 2007)

2 Explanations for serial murder

Holmes and DeBurger (1988) and Holmes and Holmes (1998) offer four typologies:

    i. visionary (describe)

    ii. missionary

    iii. hedonistic

    iv. power/control

3 Other factors – biological

    i. genetic factors

    ii. head trauma

    iii. abnormal brain activity

4 Other factors – psychological

    i. psychosis (Hickey, 1997)

    ii. psychopath (Hare, 1993)

5 Other factors – sociological

    i. Leyton (1989) – serial killing as social protest

    ii. Wilson (2007) – we should forget the killers, but recognize the vulnerability of victims

Conclusion

Which explanations are convincing (if any)? Why are they convincing?

SELECTING PERTINENT TOPICS

When you are constructing a draft outline for an essay or project, you should ask what the major question(s) are that you wish to address, or which topics are pertinent to the subject. It would be useful to make a list of all the issues that spring to mind that you might wish to tackle. The ability to design a good question is an art form that should be cultivated, and such questions will allow you to impress your assessor with the quality of your thinking.

To illustrate the point, consider the example presented below. If you were asked to write an essay about the effectiveness of the police in your local community you might, as your starting point, pose the following questions.

The effectiveness of the police in the local community: Initial questions

- Is there a high profile police presence?
- Are there regular 'on the beat' officers and patrol car activities?
- Do recent statistics show increases or decreases in crime in the area?
- Are the police involved in community activities and local schools?
- Does the local community welcome and support the police?
- Do the police have a good reputation for responding to calls?
- Do the police harass people unnecessarily?
- Do minority groups perceive the police as fair?
- Do the police have an effective complaints procedure to deal with grievances against them?
- Do the police solicit and respond to local community concerns?

REST YOUR CASE

It should be your aim to give the clear impression that your arguments are not based entirely on hunches, bias, feelings or intuition. In exams and essay questions it is usually assumed (even if not directly specified) that you will appeal to evidence to support your claims. Therefore, when you write your essay, you should ensure that it is liberally sprinkled with citations and evidence. By the time the assessor reaches the end of your work, he or she should be convinced that your conclusions are evidence-based. A flaw to be avoided is to make claims for which you have provided no authoritative source.

> You should convey a clear impression that what you have asserted is derived from relevant sources (including sources that are up to date). It looks better in terms of presentation if you spread your citations across your essay rather than compressing them into a paragraph or two at the end. Indeed if you are looking to show knowledge that has been gained through wider reading and study, you should produce an essay that is punctuated with citations. Good examples of presentation can be found in academic journals.

Some examples of how you might introduce your evidence and sources are provided below:

According to Young (2007) …

Garland (2002) has concluded that …

Winlow (2001) found that …

It has been claimed by Wilson and O'Sullivan (2004) that …

Hall (2012) has asserted that …

It is sensible to vary the expression used so that you are not monotonous and repetitive, and it also aids variety to introduce researchers' names at various places in the sentence (not always at the beginning). It is advisable to choose the expression that is most appropriate – for example, you can make a stronger statement about reviews that have identified recurrent and predominant trends in findings as opposed to one study that appears to run contrary to all the rest.

CAREFUL USE OF QUOTATIONS

Although it is desirable to present a good range of cited sources, it is not judicious to present these as a 'patchwork quilt', i.e. you just paste together what others have said with little thought for interpretative comment or coherent structure. It is a good general point to aim to avoid very lengthy quotes – short ones can be very effective. Aim at blending the quotations as naturally as possible into the flow of your sentences. Also, it is good to vary your practices – sometimes use short, direct, brief quotes (cite page number as well as author and year), and at times you can summarize the gist of a quote in your own words. In this case you should cite the author's name and year of publication but leave out quotation marks and page number.

In terms of referencing, practice may vary from one discipline to the next, but some general points that will go a long way in contributing to good practice are as follows:

- If a reference is cited in the text, it must be in the list at the end (and vice-versa).
- Names and dates in the text should correspond exactly with the list in your References or Bibliography.
- The list of References and Bibliography should be in alphabetical order by the surname (not the initials) of the author or first author.
- Any reference you make in the text should be traceable by the reader (they should clearly be able to identify and trace the source).
- Accurate referencing is important, and failure to accurately reference can impact upon your marks.
- Every institution will have guidelines available, and seeking these out will help you appreciate the accepted convention for your course.

KNOWING ABOUT PLAGIARISM AND AVOIDING IT

In all aspects of academic study and research, concepts and ideas inescapably build on those of other researchers and theorists – indeed this is a legitimate and essential part of scholarship. Plagiarism is the taking and using as one's own the thoughts, writings, or inventions of another, but in an academic context, plagiarism implies a dishonest, intentional deliberate act on the part of the writer or researcher to use the work, ideas or expressions of others as if they were his or her own.

Deliberate plagiarism, therefore, is academic cheating, and universities have a very firm view on this: anyone found to have deliberately copied or plagiarized the work of others (be it academic works or the work of another student or person) will be severely penalized. Some people do try to cheat, say by buying essays online, but most universities have developed sophisticated technological systems that can detect this. Deliberate plagiarism with a clear intention to cheat is, in my experience, far less common than plagiarism that is committed through misunderstanding, thoughtlessness or even carelessness. These latter types of plagiarism occur when students fail to acknowledge fully the sources of knowledge and ideas that they use in their work, incorporate the words of others into their writing as if they were their own and do not reference properly, and when students piece together ideas or facts taken from notes and lecture notes that they have not kept with sufficient care. Many students, particularly those at the beginning of their courses, are unclear about how to use the work of others in a way that may not constitute intentional plagiarism, but may be regarded instead as poor academic practice (most universities impose lesser penalties for such offences, but poor academic practice is often still penalized). However, with some planning and preparation it is possible to avoid putting yourself at risk of plagiarism.

Understanding how to use and appropriately acknowledge your debt to the work of others is an essential step in learning how to avoid plagiarism. Making sure that when you are reading or researching for any work, you include in your notes, or on any photocopies, the full reference details of each source that you use is one thing you can do that will help you avoid plagiarism, as this will ensure that you have all the information you need to acknowledge your sources fully when you come to use this material in your work.

When you write down the precise words of a writer, or even of a lecturer, make sure that you mark clearly in your notes that you have included an exact quotation, and add the relevant page number to the other reference details (this includes the citation of sources on the internet, and online discussion lists/mail bases/databases). Getting into such good study practices will ensure that when you go back to your notes at a later date you will be able distinguish your own words from those of your sources. Simple things like writing in different coloured inks can help, or carrying a highlighter and always highlighting material that is not your own original work can help too. An appropriate sentence or phrase quoted from an expert in the field can be used with great effect within an essay or dissertation, but it needs to be fully referenced and clearly distinguished from your own words. If you do this, make sure that you carefully reference and acknowledge sources and avoid plagiarism.

A CLEARLY DEFINED INTRODUCTION

In an introduction to an essay you have the opportunity to define the problem or issue that is being addressed and to set it within context. Resist the temptation to elaborate on any issue at the introductory stage. What you should aim to do in the introduction is to provide the essence of what will follow in order to set a context. To this end, it is far better to be succinct and leave the reader wanting to read further.

Exercise

An example for practice, if you wish: look back at the drafted outline on serial killers (pages 144–145). Try to design an introduction for that essay in about 300 words. Alternatively, choose a sample question from the end of this chapter, or any of the core areas of the curriculum, and write an introduction.

CONCLUSION – ADDING THE FINISHING TOUCHES

In the conclusion you should aim to tie your essay together in a clear and coherent manner. It is your last chance to leave an overall impression in your reader's mind. Therefore, you will at this stage want to do justice to your efforts and not sell yourself short. This is your opportunity to identify where the strongest evidence points or where the balance of probability lies. The conclusion to an exam question often has to be written hurriedly under the pressure of time, but with an essay (coursework) you have time to reflect on, refine and adjust the content to your satisfaction. It should be your goal to make the conclusion a smooth finish that does justice to the range of content in summary and succinct form. Do not underestimate the value of an effective conclusion. 'Sign off' your essay in a manner that brings closure to the treatment of your subject.

TOP DOWN AND BOTTOM UP CLARITY

An essay gives you the opportunity to refine each sentence and paragraph on your computer. Each sentence is like a tributary that leads into the stream of the paragraph that in turn leads into the main stream of the essay. From a 'top down' perspective (i.e. starting at the top with your major outline points), clarity is facilitated by the structure you draft in your outline. You can ensure that the subheadings are appropriately placed under the most relevant main heading, and that both sub and main headings are arranged in logical sequence. From a 'bottom up' perspective (i.e. building up the details that 'flesh out' your main points), you should check that each sentence is a 'feeder' for the predominant concept in a given paragraph. When all this is done you can check that the transition from one point to the next is smooth rather than abrupt.

Checklist: Summary for essay writing

✓ Before you start, have a 'warm up' by tossing the issues around in your head.
✓ List the major concepts and link them in fluent form.
✓ Design a structure (outline) that will facilitate balance, progression, fluency and clarity.
✓ Pose questions and address these in critical fashion.
✓ Demonstrate that your arguments rest on evidence and spread cited sources across your essay.
✓ Provide an introduction that sets the scene and a conclusion that rounds off the arguments.

Checklist: Attempt to write (or at least think about) some additional features that would help facilitate good essay writing:

✓ ....
✓ ....
✓ ....
✓ ....
✓ ....

In the above checklist you could have features such as originality, clarity in sentence and paragraph structure, applied aspects, addressing a subject you feel passionately about and the ability to avoid going off on a tangent.

3.6   REVISION HINTS AND TIPS

This chapter will help you to:

- map out your accumulated material for revision
- choose summary tags to guide your revision
- keep well-organized folders for revision
- make use of effective memory techniques
- revise in a way that combines bullet points and in-depth reading
- profit from the benefits of revising with others
- attend to the practical exam details that will help keep panic at bay
- use strategies that keep you task-focused during the exam
- select and apply relevant points from your prepared outlines.

START AT THE BEGINNING

Strategy for revision should be on your mind from your first lecture at the beginning of your academic semester. You should be like the squirrel that stores up nuts for the winter. Do not waste any lecture, tutorial, seminar, group discussion etc. by letting the material evaporate into thin air. Get into the habit of making a few guidelines for revision after each learning activity. Keep a folder, or file, or little notebook that is reserved for revision and write out the major points that you have learned. By establishing this regular practice you will find that what you have learned becomes consolidated in your mind, and you will also be in a better position to 'import' and 'export' your material both within and across subjects.

COMPILE SUMMARY NOTES

It would be useful and convenient to have a little notebook or cards on which you can write outline summaries that provide you with an overview of your subject at a glance. You could also use treasury tags to hold different batches of cards together whilst still allowing for inserts and resorting. Such practical resources can easily be slipped into your pocket or bag and produced when you are on the bus or train or whilst sitting in a traffic jam. They would also be useful if you are standing in a queue or waiting for someone who is not in a rush! A glance over your notes will consolidate your learning and will also activate your mind to think further about your subject. Therefore it would also be useful to make note of the questions that you would like to think about in greater depth. Your primary task is to get into the habit of constructing outline notes that will be useful for revision.

KEEP ORGANIZED RECORDS

People who have a fulfilled career have usually developed the twin skills of time and task management. It is worth pausing to remember that you can use your academic training to prepare for your future career in this respect. Therefore, ensure that you do not fall short of your potential because these qualities have not been cultivated. One important tactic is to keep a folder for each subject and divide this topic by topic. You can keep your topics in the same order in which they are presented in your course lectures. Bind them together in a ring binder or folder and use subject dividers to keep them apart. Make a numbered list of the contents at the beginning of the folder, and list each topic clearly as it marks a new section in your folder. Another important practice is to place all your notes on a given topic within the appropriate section – don't put off this simple task, do it straightaway. Notes may come from lectures, seminars, tutorials, internet searches, personal notes, etc. It is also essential that when you remove these for consultation, you return them to their 'home' immediately after use.

The most important point here is that you will have gathered a wide variety of material that should be organized in such a way that will allow you to use a range of evidence to come up with some satisfactory and authoritative conclusions. Being organized will help you toward your end goal, whereas poor organization will hinder you.

USE PAST PAPERS

Revision will be very limited if it is confined to memory work. You should, by all means, read over your revision cards or notebook and keep the picture of the major facts in front of your mind's eye. However, it is also essential that you become familiar with previous exam papers so that you will have some idea of how the questions are likely to be framed. Therefore, build up a good range of past exam papers (especially recent ones) and add these to your folder.

It is very unlikely that in examinations the questions that you are asked will be abstract, or cover a subject in a wholly different way, though it is possible that this may be the case. You can prepare yourself mentally, to a degree, by running over what you might be asked in your mind, and thinking about how best you might answer. Such a trick is a transferable skill that you can also apply to job interviews!

"Evaluate the advantages and disadvantages of allowing private for profit companies to deliver criminal justice interventions. (Note: this should not be seen as an extensive list but rather as an example of some of the issues.)"

Immediately you can see that you will require two lists and you can begin to work on documenting your reasons under each, as below:

Table 3.2

Advantages	Disadvantages
• The introduction of private sector competition improves standards in state sector, some argue it has done this in prisons	• The state arrests and prosecutes, and therefore also has a moral responsibility to punish
• Private companies can provide an effective means of increasing innovation, and can provide up front investment that can reduce the burden on the tax payer	• Pay and conditions in private sector may compare unfavourably with state run organizations and this has 'knock on' effects in terms of staff quality and moral
• There is a need for more flexibility on the part of the CJS and private companies are often more flexible and adaptable	• Private for profit organizations cost savings can drive standards down and prioritize shareholders rather than the social good
• There are some examples where private companies can raise efficiency and reduce costs	• In the long term, private companies are often no more profitable and end up being subsidized by the state
• Economically free competition in the market place spurs efficiency and quality of service	• Private companies have a desire to make profit; can provide less in terms of staff, regimes, etc.
• Moral arguments about the role of private companies and their desire to make profits should actually be secondary to delivery of an effective CJS as this is what concerns the public more. There is some evidence that privatization is effective	• Letting private companies into the CJS introduces a profit incentive and a powerful group with vested interests in expanding social control, rather than finding other effective solutions

You will have also noticed that the word 'evaluate' is in the question – so your mind must go to work on making judgements. You may decide to work through disadvantages first and then through advantages, or it may be your preference to compare, point by point, as you go along. Whatever conclusion you come to may be down to personal, subjective opinion but at least you will have worked through all the issues from both standpoints. The lesson is to ensure that part of your revision should include critical thinking as well as memory work.

EMPLOY EFFECTIVE MNEMONICS (MEMORY AIDS)

The Greek word from which 'mnemonics' is derived refers to a tomb – a structure that is built in memory of a loved one, friend or respected person. 'Mnemonics' can be simply defined as aids to memory – devices that will help you recall information that might otherwise be difficult to retrieve from memory. For example, if you find an old toy in the attic of your house, it may suddenly trigger a flood of childhood memories associated with it. Mnemonics can therefore be thought of as keys that open your memory's storehouse.

Visualization is one technique that can be used to aid memory. For example, the **location method** is where a familiar journey is visualized and you can 'place' the facts that you wish to remember at various landmarks along the journey, for example a bus stop, a car park, a shop, a store, a bend, a police station, a traffic light, etc. This has the advantage of making an association of the information you have to learn with other material that is already firmly embedded and structured in your memory. Therefore, once the relevant memory is activated, a dynamic 'domino effect' will be triggered. However, there is no reason why you cannot use a whole toolkit of mnemonics. As well as the location method defined above, some other examples and illustrations of mnemonics are presented below.

Visualization – Turn information into pictures. Some people find that their memory is stimulated by visualizing an image – an example might be to read Lombroso's *Criminal Man* (1876) and try to visualize a picture of what such a criminal might look like; remember the features of atavism that Lombroso sets out. You may then be able to recall more than if you tried just to read and memorize text.

Peg system – 'Hang' information onto a term so that when you hear the term you will remember the ideas connected with it (an umbrella term). In the example on typologies of serial killers there are four different types: visionary, missionary, hedonistic and power control. Under visionary you could remember key features of this type, e.g. hallucinations, inner voices, random victim selection, disorganization.

Hierarchical system – This is a development of the previous point with higher-order, middle-order and lower-order terms. For example, you could think of the continents of the world (higher order), and then group these into the countries under them (middle order). Under countries you could then have cities, rivers and mountains (lower order).

Acronyms – Take the first letter of all the key words and make a word from these; some people find this a useful aid to memory. In criminology and criminal justice studies acronyms are quite frequently used, for example, the anti-social behaviour order becomes the ASBO.

Mind maps – These have become very popular – they allow you to draw lines that stretch out from the central idea and to develop the subsidiary ideas in the same way. It is a little like the pegging and hierarchical methods combined and turned sideways. The method has the advantage of giving you the complete picture at a glance, although they can become a complex work of art!

Rhymes – Words that rhyme and words that end with a similar sound (e.g. commemoration, celebration, anticipation). These provide another dimension to memory work by including sound. Memory can be enhanced when information is processed in various modalities, for example, hearing, seeing, speaking, visualizing.

ALTERNATE BETWEEN METHODS

It is not sufficient to present outline points in response to an exam question (although it is better to do this than nothing if you have run out of time in your exam). Your aim should be to put 'meat on the bones' by adding substance, evidence and arguments to your basic points. You should work at finding the balance between the two methods – outline revision cards might be best reserved for short bus journeys, whereas extended reading might be better employed for longer revision slots at home or in the library. Your ultimate goal should be to bring together an effective, working approach that will enable you to face your exam questions comprehensively and confidently.

REVISING WITH OTHERS

If you can find a few other students to revise with, this will provide another fresh approach to the last stages of your learning. First ensure that others carry their workload and are not merely using the hard work of others as a short cut to success. Of course you should think of group sessions as one method, but it is not the only method. A collective approach will allow you to assess your strengths and weaknesses (showing you where you are off track), and to benefit from the resources and insights of others, but some people *do* revise more effectively on their own, without distractions. If you do revise with others, try to design some questions for the whole group to address before you meet. It is also worth making this a task for other group members. The group could also go through past exam papers and discuss the points that might provide an effective response to each question. It should not be the aim of the group to provide standard and identical answers for each group member to mimic. Group work is currently deemed to be advantageous by educationalists, and team work is held to be a desirable employability quality.

Checklist: Good study habits for revision time

- ✓ Set a date for the 'official' beginning of revision and prepare for 'revision mode'.
- ✓ Do not force cramming by leaving revision too late.
- ✓ Take breaks from revision to avoid saturation.
- ✓ Indulge in relaxing activities to give your mind a break from pressure.
- ✓ Minimize or eliminate use of alcohol during the revision season.
- ✓ Get into a good rhythm of sleep to allow renewal of your mind.
- ✓ Avoid excessive caffeine especially at night so that sleep is not disrupted.
- ✓ Try to adhere to regular eating patterns.
- ✓ Try to have a brisk walk in fresh air each day (for example, in the park).
- ✓ Avoid excessive dependence on junk food and snacks.

3.7   EXAM TIPS

This chapter will help you to:

- develop strategies for controlling your nervous energy
- tackle worked examples of time and task management in exams
- attend to the practical details associated with the exam
- stay focused on the exam questions
- link revision outlines to strategy for addressing exam questions.

HANDLING YOUR NERVES

Exam nerves are not unusual and it has been concluded that test anxiety arises because of the perception that your performance is being evaluated, that the consequences are likely to be serious and that you are working under the pressure of a time restriction. However, if you focus on the task at hand rather than on feeding a downward negative spiral in your thinking patterns, this will help you keep your nerves under control. Proper preparation will also help you, as the best way to avoid stress is to put in the necessary study hours. If you are well prepared, know your subject and have put in a good amount of work, your biggest worry really should be making sure that your answers reflect the work you have done. I am not denying that exams can be worrying and can induce stress, but good preparation and knowing your subject will make you more confident even if you are prone to exam anxieties.

TIME MANAGEMENT WITH EXAMPLES

The all-important matter as you approach an exam is to develop the belief that you can take control over the situation. As you work through the list of issues that you need to address, you will be able to tick them off one by one. One of the issues you will need to be clear about before the exam is the length of time you should allocate to each question. Sometimes this can be quite simple (although it is always necessary to read the rubric carefully), for example, if two questions are to be answered in a two-hour paper, you should allow one hour for each question. If it is a two-hour paper with one essay question and five shorter answers, you could allow one hour for the essay and 12 minutes each for the shorter questions. However, you always need to check out the weighting for the marks on each question, and you will also need to deduct whatever time it takes you to read over the paper and to choose your questions.

Common pitfall

Too many students make basic mistakes in exams because they fail at the simplest of tasks. Remember to check the time limit on the paper, to allocate time accordingly between questions, and then stick to timings. Also, although it sounds like common sense, read the questions thoroughly and make sure that you are certain what you are being asked. Frequently students limit their marks by falling into common traps. Do not allow yourself to make this mistake.

After you have decided on the questions you wish to address, you then need to plan your answers. Some students prefer to plan all outlines and draft work at the beginning, whilst others prefer to plan and address one answer before proceeding to address the next question. Decide on your strategy before you enter the exam room and stick to your plan. When you have done your draft outline as rough work, you should allocate an appropriate time for each section. This will prevent you from excessive treatment of some aspects whilst falling short on other parts. Such careful planning will help you achieve balance, fluency and symmetry.

Common pitfall

Some students put as much effort into their rough work as they do into their exam essay, but if this is not allowed to be marked, is there any purpose? These are issues where you must decide upon the necessary balance, and find the position where you feel adequately prepared given the time constraints. You do not want to limit your marks because too much time was spent on the plan.

EXERCISE

Discuss whether it is justifiable to criminalize cannabis.
1   Arguments for criminalization
    i. Cannabis is harmful
    ii. The majority of the public do not smoke cannabis
    iii. Criminalization is the only effective means of showing society's disapproval and preventing people from using
    iv. Cannabis can be harmful to health and mental health, even if other drugs are legal
2   Some arguments against criminalization
    i. There are far more harmful forms of drug such as alcohol and tobacco, and these are legal
    ii. Criminalization wastes criminal justice time and resources
    iii. Youths who are given a 'cannabis caution' for minor possession offences can find it difficult to find a job
    iv. Criminalization and the war on drugs has failed to cut drug usage, but has filled our jails, cost tax payers money and fuelled organized crime
3   Qualifying suggestions
    i. Personal possession decriminalized
    ii. Follow the Dutch (Amsterdam coffee shop model) or system in California, USA

CONTROL WANDERING THOUGHTS

When in your exams, try to keep to task. Again this may sound like common sense but it is true to suggest that one way you may fail your exam is to get up and walk out of the test room without writing anything; another way is to 'leave' the test room mentally by being preoccupied with distracting thoughts. The distracting thoughts may be either related to the exam itself or totally irrelevant to it. The net effect of both these forms of intrusion is to distract you from the task at hand and debilitate your test performance.

Research has consistently shown that distracting, intrusive thoughts during an exam are more detrimental to performance than stressful symptoms such as sweaty palms, dry mouth, tension, trembling, etc. Moreover, it does not matter whether the distracting thoughts are negative evaluations related to the exam or are totally irrelevant to the exam. The latter may be a form of escape from the stressful situation.

PRACTICAL SUGGESTIONS FOR CONTROLLING WANDERING THOUGHTS

- Be aware that this problem is detrimental to performance.
- Do not look around to find distractions.
- If distracted, write down 'keep focused on task'.
- If distracted again, look back at your 'keep focused' instruction and continue to do this.
- Start to draft rough work as soon as you can.
- If you struggle with initial focus then reread or elaborate on your rough work.
- If you have started your essay reread your last paragraph (or two).
- Do not throw fuel on your distracting thoughts – starve them by re-engaging with the task at hand.

LINKS TO REVISION

If you have followed the guidelines given for revision, you will be well equipped with outline plans when you enter the exam room. You may have chosen to use headings and subheadings, mind maps, hierarchical approaches or just a series of simple mnemonics. Whatever method you choose to use, you should be furnished with a series of memory triggers that will trigger memory for you once you begin to write. You also might want to restrict your focus to, say, three or four subjects that you feel most comfortable and familiar with, although of course this will depend upon circumstance and what is required of you.

THE ART OF 'NAME DROPPING'

In most topics at university you will be required to cite studies as evidence for your arguments and to link these to the names of researchers, scholars or theorists. It will help if you can use the correct dates or at least the decades, and it is good to demonstrate that you have used contemporary sources, and have done some independent work. A marker will have dozens if not hundreds of scripts to work through and they will know if you are just repeating the same phrases from the same sources as everyone else. There is inevitably a certain amount of this that must go on, but there is room for you to add fresh and original touches that demonstrate independence and imagination.

Convey the impression that you have done more than the bare minimum and that you are enthusiastic about criminology. Like essay writing, use citations to support arguments (you may even be able to remember some brief quotations). There is no reason why an examination essay should adopt a format that is radically different to that of a written essay. Try to spread researchers' and theorists' names across your exam essay rather than compressing them into, for example, the first and last paragraphs.

A POLITICIAN'S ANSWER

Politicians are renowned for refusing to answer questions directly or for evading them through raising other questions. A humorous example is when a politician was asked, 'Is it true that you always answer questions by asking another?' The reply given was, 'Who told you that?'

The message here is to make sure that you answer the set question, although there may be other questions that arise out of this for further study that you might want to highlight in your conclusion. As a first principle you must answer the set question and not another question that you had hoped for in the exam or essay.

Table 3.3   Discuss justifications for seeing drugs use as a health rather than criminal justice issue

Directly relevant points	Less relevant points
• Health and psychological treatments such as cognitive behavioural therapies have been shown to work well with addicted behaviours including drug addicts	• Much drug crime is disorganized and acquisitive; and situational crime prevention may prevent it
• Replacement prescribing of heroin and methadone can prevent the need to engage in crime	• Drug users commit lots of crimes
• Such treatments can be effective, and many people believe £1 spent on treatment results in £3 less on crime	• There can be risks involved in taking drugs
• Many people believe that for treatment to be effective it should be voluntaristic rather than coercive, hence it is better viewed through the prism of health	• Prison stops some people committing crime, even temporarily
• Some forms of coercive treatment do seem to suggest, however, that they reduce drug use, and therefore related crime	• Strain theory suggests drug use might be attempts to retreat from society

Although some of the points listed in the second column of Table 3.3 may be relevant, they may be less relevant. It is part of your task to make sure that you answer the question. You can use some less relevant information, but the directly relevant points above are directly relevant because they meet the requirements of the question.

Common pitfall

Students sometimes have a wealth of information ready to draw upon, which they will write down, even when it is of little relevance to the subject under discussion. This very often results in an 'all I know about' essay that lacks structure. Try to be pertinent to the point under discussion and resist the temptation to use information that is not directly relevant to the question.

MISSING YOUR QUESTION

I have made this point before, but it is worth restating – the habit of 'question spotting' is always a risky game to play, and you should never take for granted what may appear on an exam. However, the reality is often that the question a student might be looking for is there, but they have not seen it. Some expect the question to be couched in certain words and cannot find these when they scan over the questions in blind panic. Therefore, the simple lesson is always read over the questions carefully, slowly and thoughtfully. This practice is time well spent. Also bear in mind that terms in criminology may vary. You will probably fail your exam if you revise 'right realist' criminology without knowing the exam question might ask you to critique 'neo-conservative' criminology. On such simple misunderstandings students fail exams.

WRITE IT DOWN

If you write down the question you have chosen to address, and perhaps quietly articulate it with your lips, you are more likely to process fully its true meaning and intent. Think of how easy it is to misunderstand a question that has been put to you verbally because you have misinterpreted the tone or emphasis.

PURSUE A CRITICAL APPROACH

In degree courses you are usually expected to write critically rather than merely descriptively, although it may be necessary to use some minimal descriptive substance as the raw material for your debate.

Given that most questions will require some form of critical evaluation of the evidence or theory, you should prepare to address the issues one by one from both standpoints. What you should not do is digress into a tangent about the irrelevant or abstract information (often weak students will draw upon 'I think that …' or 'common sense' arguments more suited to tabloid newspapers).

ANALYSE THE PARTS

In an effective sports team the end product is always greater than the sum of the parts. Similarly, a good essay cannot be constructed without reference to the parts. Furthermore, the parts will arise as you break down the question into the components it suggests to you. Although the breaking down of a question into components is not sufficient for an excellent essay, it is a necessary starting point.

"Trace in a critical manner western society's changing attitudes to the corporal punishment of children."

In this case you might want to consider the role of governments, the church, schools, parents and the media. However, you will need to have some reference points to the past as you are asked to address the issue of change. There would also be scope to look at where the strongest influences for change arise and where the strongest resistance comes from. You might argue that the changes have been dramatic or evolutionary, you may argue not. You might want to support your argument with reference to 'social theory', such as Norbert Elias's 'civilizing process'.

Checklist: Ensuring that questions are understood before being fully addressed

✓ Read over the chosen question several times.
✓ Write it down to ensure that it is clear.
✓ Check that you have not omitted any important aspect or point of emphasis.
✓ Ensure that you do not wrongly impose preconceived expectations on the question.
✓ Break the question into parts (dismantle and rebuild).

Checklist: Write your own checklist on any additional points of guidance for exams that you have picked up from tutors or textbooks:

✓ ....
✓ ....
✓ ....
✓ ....
✓ ....

WHEN ASKED TO DISCUSS

Students often ask how much of their own opinion they should include in an essay. In a discussion, when you raise one issue, another one can arise out of it. It is important that you recognize that your aim should be not just to identify and define all the parts that contribute, but also to show where they fit (or don't fit) into the overall picture.

Checklist: Features of a response to a 'discuss' question

✓ Contains a chain of issues that lead into each other in sequence.
✓ Clear shape and direction is unfolded in the progression of the argument.
✓ Underpinned by reference to findings and certainties.
✓ Identification of issues where doubt remains.
✓ Tone of argument may be tentative but should not be vague.

IF A CRITIQUE IS REQUESTED

One example that might help clarify what is involved in a critique is the hotly debated topic of the physical punishment of children. It would be important in the interest of balance and fairness to present all sides and shades of the argument. You would then look at whether there is available evidence to support each argument, and you might introduce issues that have been coloured by prejudice, tradition, religion and legislation. It would be an aim to identify emotional arguments, arguments based on intuition and to get down to those arguments that really have solid evidence-based support. Finally you would want to flag up where the strongest evidence appears to lie, and you should also identify issues that appear to be inconclusive. It would be expected that you should, if possible, arrive at some conclusions.

IF ASKED TO COMPARE AND CONTRAST

When asked to compare and contrast, you should be thinking in terms of similarities and differences. You should ask what the two issues share in common, and what features of each are distinct. Your preferred strategy for tackling this might be to work first through all the similarities and then through all the contrasts (or vice versa). Or, on the other hand, to work through a similarity and a contrast, followed by another similarity and contrast, etc.

"COMPARE AND CONTRAST RIGHT AND LEFT REALISM."

Similarities

• Both believed crime rates had risen from the late 1970s.
• Both thought crime to be damaging, and had real negative effects on victims and communities.

- Both believed there is the need for academic criminologists to produce research that helps to develop realistic policy that will feed into practices that counter the 'crime problem'.
- Both are more concerned with the 'crimes of the street' than 'crimes of the elites'.
- Both regard the community as a part of the solution to crime problems.

Contrasts

- They are informed by different political ideology.
- Difference in terms of perceptions about 'solutions to crime'.
- Difference of opinion as to whether crime is freely chosen.
- Divided in terms of the notion that the state should withdraw from delivery of services.

WHENEVER EVALUATION IS REQUESTED

A worked example of evaluation

"Imagine that you are a researcher asked to investigate the extent of the effect of a police pilot initiative to reduce the rate of burglary in three roads, by promoting property marking, and offering residents security advice on one inner city estate where the crime rate is high. How would you go about this?"

As part of your task you might want to review past features (retrospectively), such as, what was the previous extent of burglary. You might want to outline present features (perspective) such as the residents' views of the scheme, and envisage positive future changes (prospective). Indeed, in an evaluation you are being asked, to an extent, to select your focus (and there may be an extensive list of things that could be relevant).

This illustration may provoke you to think about how you might approach a question. If it does it has served its purpose, because generally evaluating something requires you to ask searching questions. If you encounter a question that asks you to evaluate some theory in criminology, you can draw upon the criteria for evaluating theory. If you are asked to evaluate a scheme or project you might find the following questions stimulating:

- How can I find out if this scheme/project has had an effect?
- Has the scheme/project demonstrated any effect?
- Does the scheme/project have a supportive theoretical/evidence base?
- Is this evidence robust?
- Where does it come from?
- How was it generated?
- Are there questionable elements that have been or should be challenged?
- Does more recent evidence point to a need for modification?
- Are there aspect(s) that can be improved?
- Have there been any unforeseen 'side-effects'? (For example, in relation to the above example, have the burglars just moved to new streets?)
- Could it be strengthened through being merged with other theories/concepts?

Checklist: Write your own checklist on what you remember or understand about each of the following: 'Discuss', 'Compare and Contrast', 'Evaluate' and 'Critique' (just a key word or two for each). If you find this difficult then you should read this chapter again and then try once more.

✓ ....

✓ ....

✓ ....

✓ ....

It should be noted that the words presented in the above examples might not always be the exact words that will appear on your exam script, for example, you might find 'analyse', 'outline' or 'investigate', etc. The best advice is to check over your past exam papers and familiarize yourself with the words that are most recurrent.

In summary, this chapter has been designed to give you reference points to measure where you are at in your studies, and to help you map out the way ahead in manageable increments. It should now be clear that learning should not merely be a mechanical exercise, such as just memorizing and reproducing study material. Quality learning also involves making connections between ideas, thinking at a deeper level by attempting to understand your material, and developing a critical approach to learning. However, this cannot be achieved without the discipline of preparation for lectures, seminars and exams, or without learning to structure your material (headings and subheadings) and to set each unit of learning within its overall context in your subject and programme. An important device in learning is to develop the ability to ask questions (whether written, spoken or silent). Another useful device in learning is to illustrate your material and use examples that will help make your study fun, memorable and vivid. It is useful to set problems for yourself that will allow you to think through solutions and therefore enhance the quality of your learning.

Of course, as I suggested earlier, practice makes better, and there is no substitute for practising your writing. Practise whenever you get a chance and test yourself. For example, set yourself the task of saying out loud a synopsis of a core criminology text and remember details about it – say, take Cohen's *Folk Devils and Moral Panics*, and remember when was it written, what it argues, and when it was first published. Also you might want to think about answering practice questions, and these below are a good selection that will help you develop your skills.

- Is there such a thing as 'victimless' crime?
- What do crime statistics tell us about levels of crime in society?
- How criminal can corporations be said to be?
- What do you consider the three most significant contributions to theoretical criminology in the last two decades?
- What is meant by the term 'cultural criminology'?
- To what extent and where is it possible to link gender to crime?
- What is meant by hate crime? Is it a useful term?
- Can abolition of imprisonment be regarded a serious proposal?
- How do the origins of theoretical criminology differ between the UK, USA and Europe?
- Should zemiology replace criminology?
- Do the media accurately represent crime?

When it comes to success in your study, preparation never goes amiss. It is also important to keep your subject materials in organized folders so that you can add/extract/replace materials when you need to, but proper preparation is important at every stage, from planning essays, to getting library books early enough, to undertaking your essays. This chapter has presented strategies to guide you in organizing some aspects of academic life, but they are only a guide.

Your aim should be to become an 'all round student' who engages in and benefits from all the learning activities available to you (lectures, seminars, tutorials, computing, labs, discussions, library work, etc.), and to develop all the academic and personal skills that will put you in the driving seat to academic achievement. It will be motivating and confidence building for you, if you can recognize the value of these qualities, both across your academic programme and beyond graduation to the world of work. They will also serve you well in your continued commitment to life-long learning.

PART FOUR

ADDITIONAL RESOURCES

Glossary of some key terms

Abolitionism   A term that is used to describe the theoretical opposition to imprisonment.

Actuarial/actuarialism   A term that is used to describe risk assessment and calculation techniques associated with correctional policies and treatments.

Administrative criminology   Criminology that is linked to the political administration and emerged in Britain circa 1980. It is associated with rational choice perspectives and situational crime prevention.

Aetiology   The study of the causes or origins of behaviour. Positivistic approaches in criminology are characterized by their interest in determining the aetiology of criminal acts, for example, 'the work of Lombroso was concerned with the aetiology of criminality...'

Anomie   Refers to a social condition involving individuals and society (especially at periods of transition), when norms governing social interaction are limited or cease to exist.

Atavism   A term used by Lombroso; who suggested that while most individuals evolve, some devolve, becoming primitive or 'atavistic'. These evolutionary 'throwbacks' are 'born criminals' – the most violent criminals in society.

Carceral   A term used by Foucault (1977) to describe the role of the state as it moved to using imprisonment, and its concern with disciplining and monitoring its subjects.

Classicism   A term used to describe early criminology, particularly the works of Cesare Beccaria, and the suggestion that crime is a product of free will.

Control theory   A theory associated predominantly with Travis Hirschi that suggests that weakened social bonds and a lack of social attachment can contribute to delinquency.

Corporate crime   A term that is used to refer to breaches of criminal or civil law by organizations, whether by acts or omissions, and often reflects the values and priorities of the corporation.

Crime   Not fixed or static but changes. The term 'crime' at its most basic describes an activity which breaches criminal law; however, what activity should constitute crime is fiercely contested (see Chapter 1.5).

Criminology   A term that is used to describe an eclectic range of contributions that consider in the most part the creation of law, criminal conduct and its regulation and control (law-making, law-breaking and law enforcement) but also bolstered by discussion of 'deviant' and 'delinquent' behaviour.

Critical   A term used in criminology to describe criminological works that draw upon the conflict tradition in criminology, for example, the work of Ian Taylor (1999).

Cybercrime   A term used to describe criminal and deviant activities that involve the use of new technology, most notably the internet and the world-wide web.

Dark figure   A term that is used to describe and refer to specific criminal acts that are not recorded in official crime statistics, or are not represented/ significantly under recorded (this is also sometimes referred to as invisible or hidden crime).

Delinquency   A term which is used to refer to a range of youthful misbehaviour.

Determinism   There is no single definition of determinism, but in essence it is used in criminology to counter the philosophy of free will, suggesting that individuals may be propelled towards a criminality by factors over which they have little, if any, control.

Deterrence   A strategy of punishment associated with classicism. Deterrence can either be specific, where it aims to punish the individual so that they won't commit a crime again, or general, punishing an individual to set an example to society, so that others will not commit the same crime.

Deviance   Behaviour that is disapproved of, marginal, not common or accepted, but is not in the strict sense criminal.

Deviancy amplification   A concept associated with Leslie Wilkins that describes the way that attempts to control deviant acts by the state and its agents actually have the reverse effect and increase deviance.

Differential association   A concept associated with Sutherland that suggests criminal skills are learnt and transferred in social interaction.

Differential opportunity   A theory used by Cloward and Ohlin (1960) to describe juvenile delinquency; essentially an amalgamation of differential association and strain theories.

Drift   A concept associated with subculture studies of delinquency and David Matza (1964). It describes the way that young people literally 'drift' in and out of criminality.

Epistemology   Means 'theories of knowledge' and describes beliefs about the nature of the world and how we should generate knowledge.

Ethnography   A research method drawn from anthropology and the study of people and groups in their natural setting. Typically this involves the researcher spending prolonged periods of time with a group in order to gather data about their day-to-day activities. As a research method it is associated with the Chicago School of Sociology.

Feminism   A term used to describe perspectives that share a concern with the inequality of women and discrimination against them, by assuming that theories about male behaviour are applicable to the experiences of women.

Folk devil   A term that is used to describe those who are the subjects of moral panics and popular myths.

Freewill   The notion that people actively choose their behaviour, and are not determined by factors beyond their control. It is the theoretical basis of works in the classical tradition in criminology, but also informs right realist and administrative criminology.

Governmentality   A term that is used to describe an approach in criminology that focuses upon the way in which the state government is both planned and operates technically by responding to problems that are to be governed.

Hegemony   A term used by sociologists to describe how the domination of one class over others is achieved. In criminology it is a term that is often used by masculinity theorists.

Hidden crime   Refers to crimes, or categories of crime that are not found in official crime statistics (see Dark figure).

Incapacitation   Refers to a theory of punishment that is concerned with limiting the offender's ability to commit further crime.

Moral panic   A term coined by Cohen to describe disproportionate reaction to a perceived threat to society's values, particularly involving media representation and exaggeration which creates a public appetite for increased regulation and social control.

Organizational crime   A term that refers to corporate crime or criminality involving supposedly legitimate organizations.

Organized crime   A term used to describe serious and often collective criminality that is difficult to control, but presents a specific threat to the autonomy and power of the state.

Panopticon   Stemming from Jeremy Bentham's prison design, the term refers to a condition of observational visibility, inspection (and therefore control) that has spread into society more generally concerned with regulation; the 'carceral' society (Foucault, 1977).

Positivism   A theoretical approach that emerged during the early nineteenth century which argued that it was possible to study society and social phenomena (such as crime) using methods derived from the natural sciences. In criminology it can be biological, psychological and sociological in orientation.

Qualitative methods   Involves social research inquiry concerned with human interaction and contact (often based upon interview and observation) rather than measurable data.

Quantitative methods   Describes social research inquiry associated with statistics, probability and data, and often, though not always, linked with positivistic research methods.

Realism   Describes an approach to criminology that emerged during the late 1970s and tends to be affiliated to either the political right or left, but regardless, shares a concern with rising crime rates and the damage that crime does, and argues that criminologists should exert influence upon policy by generating useful research.

Recidivism   A term used in criminology to describe re-offending, for example, 'the recidivist offender ...'.

Social disorganization   A concept associated with the Chicago School of Criminology which suggests that community breakdown and lack of attachment to society's institutions can result in criminality.

Social learning   A psychological and sociological approach that suggests that people's behaviour is influenced by the dual relationship between person and environment.

Social theory   A term that is used to describe the sometimes complicated and theoretical ideas that are used to describe social patterns and social structures.

Strain   A criminological theory associated with Robert Merton which suggests that lack of access to legitimate opportunities can result in criminality.

Subculture   Associated with attempts to study juvenile delinquency, and the way in which the values and attitudes of some young people differ from those of 'normal' society.

White collar crime   A term that is used to signify crimes that are committed by 'respectable people' in the course of their occupation.

Bibliography

Adler, F. (1975) *Sisters in Crime*. New York: McGraw Hill.

Agnew, R. (1992) 'Foundations for a general strain theory of crime and delinquency', *Criminology*, 30 (1): 47–87.

Ainsworth, P. (2001) *Offender Profiling and Crime Analysis*. Cullompton: Willan.

Amir, M. (1971) *Patterns of Forcible Rape*. Chicago: University of Chicago Press.

Beccaria, C. (1963 [1764]) *On Crimes and Punishments*. New York: Bobbs-Merill.

Becker, H. (1963) *Outsiders: Studies in the sociology of deviance*. New York: Free Press.

Becker, H. (1964) *The Other Side: Perspective on deviance*. New York: Free Press.

Beirne, P. and South, N. (eds) (2007) *Issues in Green Criminology: Confronting harms against environments, humanity and other animals*. Cullompton: Willan.

Blackstone, W. (1856 [1756]) *A Treatise on the Laws of England*. London: W.G. Benning & Co.

Bonger, W. (1916) *Criminality and Economic Conditions*. Boston: Little, Brown.

Bonger, W. (1936) *An Introduction to Criminology*. London: Methuen and Co.

Bowling, B. (1999) *Violent Racism: Victimisation policing and social context*. Oxford: Oxford University Press.

Bowling, B. and Phillips, C. (2002) *Race, Crime and Justice*. London: Longman.

Box, S. (1983) *Power, Crime and Mystification*. London: Tavistock.

Braithwaite, J. (1989) *Crime, Shame and Reintergration*. Cambridge: Cambridge University Press.

Braithwaite, J. (2001) *Restorative Justice and Responsive Regulation*. Oxford: Oxford University Press.

Bridgeman, C. and Hobbs, L. (1997) *Preventing Repeat Victimisation: The police officer's guide*. London: Home Office.

Carlen, P. (1983) *Women's Imprisonment*. London: Routledge and Kegan Paul.

Carlson, W.G. (1981) *The Other Price of British Oil*. London: Martin Robertson.

Cavadino, M. and Dignan, J. (2007) *The Penal System* (4th edn). London: Sage.

Chakraborti, N. and Garland, J. (2009) *Hate Crime: Impact, causes and responses*. London: Sage.

Chambliss, W. (1978) *On the Take: From petty crooks to presidents*. Bloomington: Indiana University Press.

Chapman, J. (1980) *Economic Realities and the Female Offender*. Massachusetts: Lexington Books.

Christie, N. (1986) 'The ideal victim' in E.A. Fattah (ed.) *From Crime Policy to Victim Policy*. London: Macmillan.

Christie, N. (1994) *Crime Control as Industry*. London: Routledge.

Clarke, R.V. (1997) *Situational Crime Prevention: Successful case studies* (2nd edn). New York: Harrow and Heston.

Cloward, R. and Ohlin, L. (1960) *Delinquency and Opportunity: A theory of delinquent gangs.* New York: Free Press.

Cohen, A. (1955) *Delinquent Boys: The culture of the gang.* New York: Free Press.

Cohen, S. (1972) *Folk Devils and Moral Panics.* London: McGibbon and Kee.

Connell, R.W. (1987) *Gender and Power.* Cambridge: Polity Press.

Connell, R.W. (1995) *Masculinities.* Cambridge: Polity Press.

Cornish, D. and Clarke, R.V. (eds) (1996) *The Reasoning Criminal: Rational choice perspectives on offending.* New York: Springer-Verlag.

Corriea M.E. and Bowling C. (1999) 'Veering toward digital disorder: Computer-related crime and law enforcement preparedness', *Police Quarterly*, 2 (2): 225–244.

Croall, H. (2001) *Understanding White Collar Crime.* Buckingham: Open University Press.

Crow, I. (2001) *The Treatment and Rehabilitation of Offenders.* London: Sage.

Currie, E. (1985) *Confronting Crime: An American challenge.* New York: Pantheon Books.

Currie, E. (1998) *Crime and Punishment in America.* New York: Metropolitan Books.

Daly, K. (1994) *Gender, Crime, and Punishment.* New Haven: Yale University Press.

Daly, K. and Maher, L. (1998) *Criminology at the Crossroads: Feminist readings on crime and justice.* Oxford: Oxford University Press.

Darwin, C. (1885) *The Descent of Man.* London: John Murray.

Davies, P. (2010) *Gender, Crime and Victimisation.* London: Sage.

Davies, P., Francis, P. and Greer, C. (2007) *Victims, Crime and Society.* London: Sage.

Davies, P., Francis, P. and Jupp, V. (2010) *Doing Criminological Research.* London: Sage.

Devlin, A. and Turney, B. (1999) *Going Straight.* Winchester: Waterside Press.

Downes, D. (1966) *The Delinquent Solution.* London: Routledge.

Downes, D. and Morgan, R. (1997) 'Dumping the "Hostages to fortune": The politics of law and order in Post-War Britain', in M. Maguire, R. Morgan and R. Reiner (eds) *The Oxford Handbook of Criminology* (2nd edn). Oxford: Oxford University Press.

Downes, D. and Rock, P. (2011) *Understanding Deviance* (6th edn). Oxford: Oxford University Press.

Durkheim, E. (1952 [1895]) *Suicide: A study in sociology.* London: Routledge and Kegan Paul.

Elias, N. (1994) *The Civilising Process.* Oxford: Blackwell.

Evans, K. and Jamieson, J. (eds) (2008) *Gender and Crime: A Reader.* Berkshire: Open University Press.

Eysenck, H. (1977 [1964]) *Crime and Personality.* London: Routledge and Keegan Paul.

Farrell, G. and Pease, K. (1993) *Once Bitten, Twice Bitten: Repeat victimisation and its implications for crime prevention.* London: Home Office.

Felson, M. (2002) *Crime and Everyday Life* (3rd edn). Thousand Oaks: Sage.

Felson, M. and Clarke, R.V. (1998) *Opportunity Makes the Thief: Practical theory for crime prevention.* Aldershot: Ashgate.

Ferrell, J., Hayward, K., Morrison, W. and Presdee, M. (eds) (2004) *Cultural Criminology Unleashed.* London: GlassHouse.

Ferrell, J., Hayward, K. and Young, J. (2008) *Cultural Criminology: An invitation.* London: Sage.

Ferrell, J. and Saunders, C. (eds) (1995) *Cultural Criminology.* Boston: Northeastern University Press.

Ferri, E. (1895) *Criminal Sociology*. London: T. Fisher Unwin.

Foucault, M. (1977) *Discipline and Punish*. Harmondsworth: Penguin.

Gadd, D. and Farrall, S. (2004) 'Criminal careers, desistance and subjectivity: Interpreting men's narratives of change', *Theoretical Criminology*, 8 (2): 123–56.

Gadd, D. and Jefferson, T. (2007) *Psychosocial Criminology*. London: Sage.

Gadd, D., Karstedt, S. and Messner, S. (2010) *The Sage Handbook of Criminological Research Methods*. London: Sage.

Garland, D. (2001a) *The Culture of Control: Crime and social order in contemporary society*. Oxford: Oxford University Press.

Garland, D. (ed.) (2001b) *Mass Imprisonment: Social causes and consequences*. London: Sage.

Garland, D. (2002) 'Of crimes and criminals: The development of criminology in Britain', in M. Maguire, R. Morgan and R. Reiner (eds) *The Oxford Handbook of Criminology* (3rd edn). Oxford: Oxford University Press.

Goffman, E. (1961) *Asylums*. New York: Anchor.

Goffman, E. (1963) *Stigma*. New York: Simon and Schuster.

Goode, E. and Ben-Yehuda, N. (1994) *Moral Panics: The social construction of deviance*. Oxford: Blackwell.

Gottfredson, M. and Hirschi, T. (1990) *A General Theory of Crime*. Stanford: Stanford University Press.

Grabosky, P. (2001) 'Virtual criminality: Old wine in new bottles?', *Social and Legal Studies*, 10 (2): 243–249.

Green, P. and Ward, T. (2004) *State Crime: Governments, violence and corruption*. London: Pluto Press.

Greer, C. (2009) *Media and Crime: A reader*. London: Routledge.

Hale, C. et al. (2009) *Criminology*. Oxford: Oxford University Press.

Hall, S. and Jefferson, T. (1976) *Resistance through Rituals*. London: Routledge.

Hall, S., Critcher, C., Jefferson, T., Clarke, J. and Roberts, B. (1978) *Policing the Crisis: Mugging, the state and law and order*. London: Macmillan Press.

Hall, S. (2012) *Theorizing Crime and Deviance: A new perspective*. London: Sage.

Hamner, J. and Saunders, S. (1984) *Well Founded Fear: Community study of violence to women*. London: Harper Collins.

Hare, R. (1993) *Without Conscience*. London: The Guilford Press.

Harrison, J., Simpson, M., Harrison, O. and Martin, E. (2012) *Study Skills for Criminology*. London: Sage.

Henry, S. and Milovanovic, D. (1996) *Constitutive Criminology: Beyond postmodernism*. London: Sage.

Herrnstein, R. and Murray, C. (1994) *The Bell Curve: Intelligence and class structure in American life*. New York: Free Press.

Hickey, E. (1997) *Serial Murders and their Victims*. Belmont: Wadsworth.

Hillyard, P., Pantazis, C., Tombs, S. and Gordon, D. (2004) *Beyond Criminology: Taking harm seriously*. London: Pluto Press.

Hirschi, T. (1969) *Causes of Delinquency*. California: University of California Press.

HMIP (2004) *Juveniles in Custody*. London: HMSO.

Holmes, R.M. and DeBurger, J. (1988) *Serial Murder*. Newbury Park: Sage.

Holmes, R.M. and Holmes, S.T. (1998) *Serial Murder*. London: Sage.

Hope, T. (2009) 'What do crime statistics tell us?' in C. Hale, K. Hayward, A. Wahadin and E. Wincup (eds) *Criminology* (2nd edn). Oxford: Oxford University Press.

Jewkes, Y. (ed.) (2007) *Handbook of Prisons*. Cullompton: Willan.

Jewkes, Y. (2010) *Media and Crime*. London: Sage.

Jewkes, Y. and Leatherby, G. (2002) *Criminology: A reader*. London: Sage.

Jones, T., MacLean, B. and Young, J. (1986) *The Islington Crime Survey*. Aldershot: Gower.

Johnson, J., Kerper, H., Hayes D. and Killinger, G. (1973) 'The recidivist victim: A descriptive study', *Criminal Justice Monograph*, 4 (l). Huntsville: Sam Houston University.

Katz, J. (1988) *The Seductions of Crime: Moral and sensual attractions in doing evil*. New York: Basic Books.

Kiger, K. (1990) 'The darker figure of crime: The serial murder enigma', in S. Egger (ed.) *Serial Murder: An elusive phenomenon*. New York: Praeger.

Kinsey, R. (1985) *Merseyside Crime and Police Survey Final Report*. Edinburgh: University of Edinburgh.

Lange, J. (1931) *Crime as Destiny*. London: Allen and Unwin.

Laycock, G. (2005) 'Defining Crime Science', in M.J. Smith and N. Tilley (eds) *Crime Science: New approaches to preventing and detecting crime*. Cullompton: Willan.

Lea, J. and Young, J. (1984) *What is to be Done about Law and Order?* Harmondsworth: Penguin.

Lemert, E. (1972) *Human Deviance, Social Problems, Social Control*. NJ: Prentice Hall.

Lemert, E. (1997) *The Trouble with Evil: Social control at the edge of morality*. Albany: SUNY Press.

Leyton, E. (1989) *Hunting Humans: The rise of the modern multiple murderer*. Harmondsworth: Penguin.

Lombroso, C. (1876) *L'Uomo Delinquente*. Milan: Hoepli.

Lombroso, C. and Ferrero, W. (1895) *The Female Offender*. London: Fisher Unwin.

Macpherson, W. (1999) *The Stephen Lawrence Inquiry*. London: The Stationery Office.

Maguire, M. (2002) 'Crime Statistics: The "data explosion" and its implications', in M. McGuire, R. Morgan and R. Reiner (eds) *The Oxford Handbook of Criminology*. Oxford: Oxford University Press.

Maguire, M., Morgan, R. and Reiner, R. (1997) *The Oxford Handbook of Criminology* (2nd edn). Oxford: Oxford University Press.

Marshall, T. (1999) *Restorative Justice*. London: Home Office.

Martinson, R. (1974) 'What Works? Questions and answers about prison reform', *The Public Interest*, 35: 22–54.

Matza, D. (1964) *Delinquency and Drift*. London: Wiley.

Matza, D. (1969) *Becoming Deviant*. Englewood Ciffs, NJ: Prentice Hall.

Mawby, R. and Walklate, S. (1994) *Critical Victimology*. London: Sage.

May, T. (2001) *Social Research: Issues, methods and processes*. Buckingham: Open University Press.

Mayhew, P. (2000) 'Researching the State of Crime: Local, national and international victim surveys', in R.D. King and E. Wincup (eds) *Doing Research on Crime and Justice*. Oxford: Oxford University Press.

Mays, J. (1954) *Growing Up in the City*. Liverpool: Liverpool University Press.

McGuire, J. and Priestley, P. (1995) 'Reviewing what works' in J. McGuire (ed.) *What Works*. Chichester: John Wiley.

McLaughlin, E. and Muncie, J. (2001) *The Sage Dictionary of Criminology*. London: Sage.

McLaughlin, E., Muncie, J. and Hughes, G. (2003) *Criminological Perspectives: Essential readings*. London: Sage.

McRobbie, A. and Thornton, S. (1995) 'Rethinking "moral panic" for multi-mediated social worlds', *British Journal of Sociology*, 46 (4): 559–74.

Merton, R. (1938) 'Social structure and anomie', *American Sociological Review*, 3: 672–82.

Merton, R. (1968) *Social Theory and Social Structure*. New York: Free Press.

Messerschmidt, J. (1993) *Masculinity and Crime*. Boston: Rowman and Littlefield.

Michael, J. and Adler, M. (1933) *Crime, Law and Social Science*. New York: Harcourt Brace Jovanovich.

Michalowski, R. (1985) *Order, Law and Crime*. New York: Random House.

Minkes, J. and Minkes, L. (eds.) (2008) *Corporate and White Collar Crime*. London: Sage.

Morrison, W. (1995) *Theoretical Criminology*. London: Routledge.

Muncie, J. (2000) 'Decriminalising criminology' in G. Lewis, G. Gewirtz and J. Clarke (eds) *Rethinking Social Policy*. London: Sage.

Muncie, J. (2009) *Youth and Crime* (3rd edn). London: Sage.

Muncie, J., Talbot, D. and Walters, R. (eds) (2009) *Crime: Local and global*. Cullompton: Willan.

Muncie, J. and Wilson, D. (eds) (2004) *The Student Handbook of Criminal Justice and Criminology*. London: Cavandish.

Murray, C. (1984) *Losing Ground*. New York: Basic Books.

Murray, C. (1990) *The Emerging Underclass*. London: Institute for Economic Affairs.

Murray, C. (1994) *Underclass: The crisis deepens*. London: Institute for Economic Affairs.

Naylor, R.T. (1997) 'Mafias, myths and markets', *Transnational Organised Crime*, 3 (3): 15–30.

Newburn, T. (2002) *Young People, Crime and Youth Justice*. Cullompton: Willan.

Newburn, T. and Stanko, E. (1995) *Just Boys Doing Business*. London: Routledge.

Parenti, C. (1999) *Lockdown America: Police and prisons in the age of crisis*. London: Verso.

Park, R., Burgess, E.W. and McKenzie, R.D. (1925) *The City*. Chicago: University of Chicago Press.

Pearson, G. (1975) *The Deviant Imagination*. London: Macmillan.

Pearson, G. (1983) *Hooligan: A history of respectable fears*. London: MacMillan.

Pepinsky, H. and Quinney, R. (eds) (1991) *Criminology as Peacemaking*. Bloomington: Indiana University Press.

Philips, A. and Chamberlain, V. (2006) *Mori Five-year Report: An analysis of youth survey data*. London: Youth Justice Board

Pollack, O. (1950) *The Criminality of Women*. New York: A.S. Barnes.

Punch, M. (1996) *Dirty Business: Exploring corporate misconduct*. London: Sage.

Quetelet, A. (1842) *A Treatise on Man*. Edinburgh: Chambers.

Quinney, R. (1970) *The Social Reality of Crime*. Boston: Little, Brown.

Quinney, R. (1974) *Critique of Legal Order: Crime control in capitalist society*. Boston: Little, Brown.

Quinney, R. (1980 [1977]) *Class, State and Crime: On the theory and practice of criminal justice*. New York: McKay.

Quinney, R. (1993) 'A life of crime: Criminology and public policy as peacemaking', *Journal of Crime and Justice*, 16: 3–9.

Radzinowicz, L. (1999) *Adventures in Criminology*. London: Routledge.

Richards, J. and Ross, S. (2002) *Convict Criminology*. Belmont: Wadsworth Publishing.

Roche, D. (2003) *Accountability in Restorative Justice*. Oxford: Oxford University Press.

Rowe, M. (2012) *Race and Crime*. London: Sage.

Schur, E. (1965) *Crimes Without Victims*. Englewood Cliffs: Prentice Hall.

Schur, E. (1973) *Radical Non-intervention*. Englewood Cliffs: Prentice Hall.

Schwendinger, H. and Schwendinger, J. (1970) 'Defenders of order or guardians of human rights', *Issues in Criminology*, 5: 123–57.

Scott, D. and Codd, H. (2010) *Controversial Issues in Prisons*. Berkshire: Open University Press.

Sellin, T. (1938) *Culture, Conflict and Crime*. New York: Social Research Council.

Shaw, C.R. (1930) *The Jack Roller: A delinquent boy's own story*. Chicago: University of Chicago Press.

Shaw, C. and McKay, H. (1942) *Juvenile Delinquency in Urban Areas*. Chicago: University of Chicago Press.

Sheptycki, J. and Wardak, A. (2005) *Transnational and Comparative Criminology*. London: GlassHouse.

Sherman, L.W. (2009) 'Evidence and liberty: The promise of experimental criminology', *Criminology and Criminal Justice*, 9 (1): 5–28.

Silverman, J. and Wilson, D. (2002) *Innocence Betrayed*. Cambridge: Polity Press.

Silvestrim, M. and Crowther-Dowey, C. (2008) *Gender and Crime*. London: Sage.

Sim, J. (2004) 'Thinking about imprisonment', in J. Muncie and D. Wilson (eds) *Student Handbook of Criminal Justice and Criminology*. London: Cavendish.

Slapper, G. and Tombs, S. (1999) *Corporate Crime*. London: Longman.

Smart, C. (1976) *Women, Crime and Criminology*. London: Routledge and Kegan Paul.

Smart, C. (1979) 'The New Female Criminal: Reality or Myth?', *British Journal of Criminology*, 19: 50–59.

Smith, P. and Natalier, K. (2004) *Understanding Criminal Justice: Sociological perspectives*. London: Sage.

Smith, R. (2003) *Youth Justice: Ideas, policy, practice*. Cullompton: Willan.

Spalek, B. (2007) *Communities, Identities and Crime*. Bristol: Policy Press.

Stanko, E. (1998) *Counting the Costs*. London: Crime Concern.

Sutherland, E.H. (1937) *The Professional Thief*. Chicago: University of Chicago Press.

Sutherland, E.H. (1939) *Principles of Criminology*. Philadelphia: Lippincott.

Sutherland, E.H. (1945) 'Is white collar crime crime?', *American Sociological Review*, 10 (2): 132–39.

Sutherland, E.H. (1949) *White Collar Crime*. New York: Dryden.

Sutherland, E.H. and Cressey, D. (1978) *Criminology* (10th edn). Philidelphia: Lippincott.

Sykes, G. and Matza, D. (1957) 'Techniques of neutralisation: A theory of delinquency', *American Sociological Review*, 22: 664.

Tappan, P. (1947) 'Who is the criminal?', *American Sociological Review*, 12: 96–102.

Tannenbaum, F. (1938) *Crime and the Community*. New York: Ginn and Co.

Taylor, I. (1999) *Crime in Context*. Cambridge: Polity Press.

Taylor, I., Walton, P. and Young, J. (1973) *The New Criminology*. London: Routledge and Kegan Paul.

Taylor, I., Walton, P. and Young, J. (1975) *Critical Criminology*. London: Routledge and Kegan Paul.

Thrasher, F. (1927) *The Gang*. Chicago: University of Chicago Press.

Tilley, N. and G. Laycock (2007) 'From crime prevention to crime science', in G. Farrell, K. Bowers, S. Johnson and M. Townsley (eds) *Imagination for Crime Prevention: Essays in honour of Ken Pease Crime Prevention Studies*. Cullompton: Willan.

Treadwell, J. (2012) 'From the car boot to booting it up? Ebay, online counterfeiting crime and the transformation of the criminal marketplace', *Criminology and Criminal Justice*, 12 (2):175–191.

Vold, G. (1958) *Theoretical Criminology*. New York: Oxford University Press.

Von Hentig, H. (1948) *The Criminal and his Victim*. New Haven: Yale University Press.

Waddington, P.A.J. (1986) 'Mugging as a moral panic: a question of proportion', *British Journal of Sociology*, 32 (2): 245–59.

Waquant, L. (2012) 'The prison is an outlaw institution', *The Howard Journal of Criminal Justice*, 51 (1): 1–15.

Walklate, S. (2004) *Gender, Crime and Criminal Justice*. Cullompton: Willan.

Walklate, S. (ed) (2007) *Handbook of Victims and Victimology*. Cullompton: Willan.

Wall, D. (2007) *Cybercrime: The transformation of crime in the information age*. Cambridge: Polity Press.

Webber, C. (2009) *Psychology and Crime*. London: Sage.

Weisburd, D., Wheeler, S., Waring, E. and Bode, N. (1991) *Crimes of the Middle Classes: White collar offenders in the federal courts*. New Haven: Yale University Press.

Westmarland, L. (2011) *Researching Crime and Justice: Tales from the field*. London: Routledge.

Wilbanks, W. (1987) *The Myth of a Racist Criminal Justice System*. Monteray: Brooks/ Cole.

Wilkins, L. (1964) *Social Deviancy*. London: Tavistock.

Williams, K. (2004) *Criminology* (5th edn). Oxford: Oxford University Press.

Wilson, D. (2007) *Serial Killers: Hunting Britains and their victims*. Winchester: Waterside.

Wilson, D. (2011) *Looking For Laura: Public criminology and hot news*. Winchester: Waterside.

Wilson, J.Q. (1975) *Thinking About Crime*. New York: Basic Books.

Wilson, D. and Ashton, J. (2001) *What Everyone in Britain Should Know about Crime and Punishment* (2nd edn). Oxford: Oxford University Press.

Wilson, J.Q. and Herrnstein, R. (1985) *Crime and Human Nature*. New York: Simon and Schuster.

Wilson, J.Q. and Kelling, G. (2003 [1982]) 'Broken windows', in E. McLaughlin, J. Muncie and G. Hughes (eds) *Criminological Perspectives: Essential readings*. London: Sage.

Wilson, D. and O'Sullivan, S. (2004) *Images of Incarceration: Representations of prison in film and television drama*. Winchester: Waterside.

Winlow, S. (2001) *Badfellas*. Oxford: Berg.

Wood, M. (2005) 'The victimisation of young people: Findings from the Crime and Justice Survey 2003', *Home Office Research Findings 246*. London: HMSO.

Woolfgang, M. (1958) *Patterns in Criminal Homicide*. Philadelphia: University of Pennsylvania Press.

Wright, G. and Hill, J. (2004) 'Victims, crime and criminal justice' in J. Muncie and D. Wilson (eds) *Student Handbook of Criminal Justice and Criminology*. London: Cavendish.

Yar, M. (2006) *Cybercrime and Society*. London: Sage

Young, J. (1971) *The Drugtakers*. London: Paladin.

Young, J. (1999) *The Exclusive Society*. London: Sage.

Young, J. (2003) 'Merton with energy, Katz with structure', *Theoretical Criminology*, 7 (3): 389–414.

Young, J. (2007) *The Vertigo of Late Modernity*. London: Sage.

Index